CASES IN MANAGERIAL ACCOUNTING

Peter J. Clarke

Department of Accountancy
University College
Dublin

GILL AND MACMILLAN

Published in Ireland by
Gill and Macmillan Ltd
Goldenbridge
Dublin 8
with associated companies in
Auckland, Dallas, Delhi, Hong Kong,
Johannesburg, Lagos, London, Manzini,
Melbourne, Nairobi, New York, Singapore,
Tokyo, Washington
© Peter J. Clarke, 1987
0 7171 1553 4
Print origination in Ireland by
Wellset, Dublin
Printed in Great Britain by
The Camelot Press, Southampton

British Library Cataloguing in Publication Data

Clarke, Peter J.
    Cases in managerial accounting.
    1. Managerial accounting — Case studies
    I.   Title
    658.1'511'0722   HF5635
    ISBN 0-7171-1553-4

CONTENTS

PREFACE

This book of cases endeavours to fill a gap in the literature available to students of managerial accounting. Once an introductory managerial accounting course has been completed, it is a logical progression to apply the various principles and techniques to acceptably realistic managerial accounting contexts. Such an application is an essential part of the learning process since knowledge is useful only when it can be applied appropriately toward some end result. This book attempts to provide a range of cases or realistic situations with which students can associate. It represents a richer and more complex set of situations in managerial accounting than those normally included in conventional textbooks. Each case puts the student in the decision-maker's role, and expects him/her to analyse situations and problems and make appropriate decisions or recommendations. It thus allows the instructor to go beyond the traditional problem-lecture method of teaching.

The collection of cases, it is hoped, span a comprehensive range of topics and difficulty levels. They attempt to cover a variety of ways in which accounting information is used by managers in different decision-making contexts. The book is suitable for advanced managerial accounting courses at undergraduate or master levels, including MBA courses. It is also suitable for those studying managerial accounting for the various professional accountancy examinations, both in Ireland and the United Kingdom. What the collection of twenty-nine cases lacks in comprehensiveness and balance is, I hope, compensated by the relevance and teachability of the various cases and their direct application to current real-life situations.

Some of the cases included are based on general experience rather than from actual business situations. These are often referred to as 'armchair' cases. What these cases lack in specific detail and background material is hopefully off-set by their direct focus on managerial accounting principles or techniques. They also provide a greater degree of realism than many abstract problems to be found in textbooks.

Other cases are drawn from actual business situations. However, proprietory information has been disguised because the individuals involved prefer to remain anonymous. In addition, some confidential cost/revenue data have been heavily distorted. Many cases have been simplified or adapted to facilitate classroom discussion on specific areas.

The cases are grouped by subject matter although this classification is inevitably arbitrary. Part 1 contains cases on the nature of managerial accounting and revenue/cost analysis for managerial decision-making.

Part 2 has cases about budgetary control, standard costing and evaluation of performance. Standard costing systems integrate with budgets and provide information for the management control process. Part 3 is concerned with different methods of cost accumulation and classification.

To be effective and enjoyable the case method requires active participation on the part of students. Learning takes place through the analysis of business situations and problems, the application of appropriate principles and techniques to available information in order to make decisions or recommendations and the discussion and constructive criticism of different viewpoints.

Students invariably prefer the case approach to learning managerial accounting than the traditional problem-lecture method. The learning experience is more realistic and hopefully will not be forgotten.

With the case method of instruction, at least two kinds of analysis are recommended. Initially the student should work alone for a short period of time, sufficient for him to reach a conclusion to the case, no matter how tentative. Secondly, after individual preparation it is advantageous to discuss conclusions in small groups. Small group discussion provides an excellent opportunity for participants to learn from one another. New approaches or insights will be presented by other participants. Important data overlooked may now be seen in a new light. In brief, small group discussion provides an unique occasion to develop powers of persuasion, receptiveness to others' ideas and critical faculties — skills which are important in any management career. In using these cases I often ask students entirely different questions than those specified in the requirement and I encourage instructors to do the same, thus extending and increasing the value of each case.

In conclusion I wish to acknowledge the generous financial support received from The Institute of Chartered Accountants in Ireland through The Irish Accountancy Educational Trust. However, they do not necessarily endorse this book and any errors or omissions are entirely my responsibility. Finally, I owe the greatest debt of all to Dorothy for her encouragement, and little Susan and Kevin for their entertainment.

PETER J. CLARKE

Part 1

Nature of managerial accounting and revenue/cost analysis for managerial decision-making

Case 1.1 The Sunshine Travel Company

Michael O'Brien, managing director of the Sunshine Travel Company, sat quietly in his Dublin office behind his cluttered desk. It was late evening, mid-week, in November 1987. O'Brien had stayed on at the office to assess the recent audited financial statements of his company for the year ended 30 September 1987. O'Brien was both astonished and depressed at the net loss of £64,900 reported for the year just ended. He did not know how it could have occurred especially since his travel firm had sold a record number of packaged continental holidays during the year, largely as a result of the unpredictable nature of yet another Irish summer. Annual turnover exceeded £11 million for the first time in the company's history. To his amazement the company didn't even get close to a break-even situation!

O'Brien was not an accountant but he didn't have to be one to realise that a loss of this magnitude threatened the survival of his travel business. The loss would have to be rectified next year but this could only be done if he understood how it occurred in the first instance. To this end he has asked your assistance and invited you to his office to discuss the matter.

You arrive at the prearranged time and are met by O'Brien. After the usual pleasantries are exchanged he comes directly to the point of your visit. 'I have just received our accounts for last year from the auditors. I'm amazed that we've made a loss and frankly I don't understand how a loss of this size could have occurred. Have a look.'

O'Brien passes a slim file across the table to you. You look at the profit and loss account which has been certified as true and fair by the auditors and is presented in the traditional financial accounting format (Exhibit 1). Apart from confirming the amount of the loss it is not particularly helpful in analysing the current situation since it is not supported by sufficiently detailed information necessary for managerial decision-making.

Exhibit 1. Profit and loss account for year ended 30 September 1987

Sales of packaged holidays		£11,324,000
Less: Operating expenses		
Accommodation in hotels	£7,582,000	
Commission	1,132,400	
Hire of chartered airplanes	918,000	
Hire of coaches	10,500	
Salaries of resort representatives	56,000	
Advertising	640,000	
Printing of brochures	300,000	
Head office: administration costs	750,000	11,388,900
Net loss for year		(64,900)

You immediately realise that to make any progress in helping O'Brien to understand the reason for the loss, it is necessary for you to grasp how the business operates and to gather some basic operating data.

O'Brien informs you that the company sells packaged holidays to a limited range of select holiday resorts on the continent — eight in total. This method of operation ensures that the company is competing at the top end of the holiday market but it also ensures that overheads are kept within reasonable limits. The holidays are all of two weeks duration in each resort as this considerably simplifies administration and travel arrangements. Some customers would prefer either a shorter or longer holiday period but generally the majority of customers are satisfied with existing arrangements. The year is divided into two seasons. The summer season lasts for a twenty-six week period commencing in April and is followed in October by a winter season of equal length.

Further questioning reveals that the eight holiday resorts are located in three different European countries. Each country is served by special chartered flights every fortnight to a convenient airport. Thus, since resorts 1, 2, and 3 are located in Italy, customers going to these resorts share a common flight to Rome airport. Similarly, resorts 4, 5 and 6 are located in southern Spain and so customers to that country fly to Malaga airport. Resorts 7 and 8 are located in Switzerland and travellers fly to Geneva. The Spanish and Italian resorts are available only during the summer season whereas Geneva is offered only during the winter months.

The price of each packaged holiday varies depending on country, resort and grade of hotel chosen. For his money the customer gets a return flight to the airport near his resort, is transported by coach to and from his hotel in his resort, and is accommodated with full board in the hotel for the fortnight. He also has the services of a local company representative who deals with customer queries and complaints and assists in any way possible.

The Sunshine Travel company's arrangements with hoteliers is on the basis that a certain amount of hotel accommodation is booked in advance of each season but it is only paid for if and when occupied. O'Brien realises that this is a generous concession obtained by his company especially since larger organisations in the travel industry, who make block bookings, must pay whether the accommodation is utilised or not. O'Brien confirms to you that the current arrangements with hoteliers is likely to continue next year, since he had developed a good, working relationship with the various hotel managers.

The number of holidays sold for each resort, the sales price (exclusive of government tax of £5 per holiday) and the cost of the two-week stay at each hotel for the financial year just ended are given in Exhibit 2. All passengers for the same resort pay the same amount. In this respect it is company policy that no allowance or discount is available for children

4

under 2 years of age. This pricing policy ensures that customers of the company are mainly single adults or mature families, which is a market segment deliberately sought after by O'Brien. It was a matter of policy that a very high standard of accommodation was offered in the resort hotels with convenient restaurants of gourmet standard normally within walking distance.

Exhibit 2

Country/ Resorts	Number of package holidays sold	Sales price of holidays (excluding tax)	Cost of hotel accommodation
Italy			
1	£1,400	£270	£85
2	600	200	45
3	200	180	40
Spain			
4	6,100	300	170
5	10,100	340	230
6	11,400	390	270
Switzerland			
7	200	500	400
8	1,400	700	650

In discussion, O'Brien explained that holidays were sold by the company itself through its Dublin office and also through travel agents around the country. Regardless of the origin of the sale, a ten per cent commission is payable based on the selling price of each holiday. This commission seeks to motivate both head office sales staff and travel agents. He argued that it is cheaper to pay a ten per cent commission to other travel agents rather than open additional sales offices around the country and thus incur greater overheads.

You ascertain that the total cost of the chartered flights during the year could be apportioned on the basis of flights to each destination. Spain has ten times the number of flights compared to both Italy and Switzerland. All flights involved daytime flying making it more convenient for holiday-makers. The total cost of coach hire could be apportioned equally among the three destinations. It was not appropriate to further apportion it among the individual resorts since the local bus companies were paid a flat sum for their services for the season, regardless of the number of customers for each resort and the number of journeys undertaken. In addition each resort had a salaried representative for the season and all were paid at the same rate. To avoid profits or losses on foreign currency transactions all contracts were in Irish punts. This arrangement was generally acceptable to foreign customers because Ireland's entry to the EMS had prevented significant foreign exchange fluctuations.

The company advertises its holidays on television and local radio and in the newspapers. In addition, a large number of coloured holiday brochures are printed each year at the start of the season, giving details of all holiday destinations, standards of accommodation, flight times and prices and are distributed free with all enquiries. Finally there are administration costs since the Dublin office has to be maintained to deal with enquiries and sales, bookings with resort hotels and a multitude of related issues.

After some thought and further discussion with O'Brien you realise that it is necessary to separately analyse the financial performance of each resort. After all, the resorts are the products which are being sold and it is in these, or some of them, that the problem must lie. The basic facts must be established in order that the problem can be understood and possible remedies considered.

REQUIREMENT

1   Prepare a revised financial statement to better highlight why the company has made a loss of £64,900 for the year ending 30 September, 1987. Explain your workings.

2   Calculate a break-even point in terms of sales revenue for the company for the year ending 30 September 1987. Clearly specify the critical assumptions underlying your calculation.

3   What actions should be considered in order to improve results next year? Why?

Case 1.2 The Alpha Department Store

It was early January 1988, Peter Allan, owner and general manager of the Alpha Department Store, was reviewing the financial results of his retail company. A recent discussion with the firm's auditors had convinced Peter that some analysis of his current trading situation was due. In this discussion Peter had learned that similar department stores were getting a three per cent plus return on sales. Since the Alpha Department Store was only returning a margin of about two per cent on sales, Peter appreciated that a review of operating performance was appropriate. In any event an annual review of the company was a good idea, his late father used to say. It would help highlight those sections that were performing at or above expectation and those sections which were performing poorly.

For accounting and administration purposes the department store is divided into three operating sections as follows, each of which is the responsibility of a section head:

Section 1   Children's clothing and footware
Section 2   Adult clothing and footware
Section 3   Household goods

It was anticipated that each operating section would have a constant gross profit margin on sales. This was attributable to company policy whereby a fixed and predetermined mark-up was added to the cost price of all products. Since section heads were partly renumerated on a commission basis they were most reluctant to grant any type of discount from selling price. In addition, pilferage was kept to a minimum as a result of a new store security surveillance system and a procedure of 'tagging' all valuable products. A tag could only be removed by the cashier and, unless removed, would automatically trigger the alarm system if the article was bought outside a particular store territory. It was also agreed by section heads that end of season 'sales' would not take place largely because it was felt that ordinary customers would postpone purchase until the special sales began. In such circumstances the company would eventually lose revenue.

The following turnover and margins were obtained in the year ended 31 December 1987:

Section	1	2	3
Turnover (inclusive of VAT)	£240,000	£171,600	£525,000
VAT rate	zero	10%	25%
Mark-up on cost	200%	100%	50%

Peter Allan realised that the current range of products was extremely limited, being confined to clothing, footware and household goods. He

7

was anxious to expand his range of products to include stationery, confectionery, toys or even a clothing boutique. He knew that his store was probably losing valuable trade to other department stores who had recently expanded their product range. He felt that new products would increase sales volume and this would improve overall store profitability. However his immediate problem was lack of space. Floor space for any additional products could only be obtained by restricting the floor space of existing sections. Additional space could not be rented economically in the locality and Peter was reluctant to move to larger premises in the suburbs of the town, since he felt that his company would lose whatever goodwill it had built up with customers. Peter admitted to himself that the introduction of a new section or sections was a real possibility but one which he would implement only after very careful consideration. The transfer of floor space from one or all of existing sections would be resisted by existing section heads so that any proposal he would make to this effect would have to be backed by very convincing arguments.

The cost figures for the current year, 1987, and their basis of allocation for management accounting purposes are contained in Exhibit 1. Allan thought that they were representative of what the store might expect to face in the forthcoming year especially since overall sales volume was expected to remain static. The consumer spending boom had failed to materialise since personal disposable income was being constantly eroded by increasing personal tax burdens. However some cost figures were likely to change. First, basic salaries of managers and employees would increase by ten per cent due to a recent national wage agreement and a decision to include all employees in a company pension scheme. Allan had contemplated reducing staff levels so as to reduce cost but had abandoned the idea on discussion with section heads. Des Broderick, head of household goods, complained, 'We can barely cope with the volume of trade at the moment. If we can't serve customers properly we will lose business. Anyway laying off staff would adversely affect our public image and staff relations.' Allan accepted this point immediately. The only other costs which were likely to change were light, heat and general advertising. Light and heat costs would increase by five per cent due to recently announced electricity price increases. General store advertising expenditure would be increased by ten per cent to facilitate a contribution to the marketing department of the local university to undertake some basic market research on behalf of the company.

Allan did not understand why costs of light and heat, store advertising and stationery were apportioned to individual sections in the manner they were. He queried his accountant on this practice and was informed, 'that is the way we've been doing it for the past few years. The system was recommended by our auditors.'

8

Exhibit 1. Costs and other operating data for 1987

	Section 1	Section 2	Section 3
Floor space occupied:	4,000 sq. ft.	3,000 sq. ft.	5,000 sq. ft.

Rates and insurance: £36,000	To be apportioned to sections on the basis of floor space occupied.
Sales commission:	Ten per cent of sales
Light and heat: £33,000	To be apportioned on the basis of floor space with a weighting of: Section 1 5 Section 2 1 Section 3 5
Store advertising: £48,000	To be apportioned as follows: Section 1 25% Section 2 10% Section 3 65%
Administration expenses:	Include interest, telephone, stationery and delivery costs amounting to £4,000 and administration salaries amounting to £23,000 for the recent accounting year. Administration cost are not allocated to a specific section since they are considered to be a general overhead.
Salaries:	One manager is employed in each section at a basic salary cost of £13,000 per annum. In addition it is company policy to employ one sales assistant, at a basic annual salary of £8,000 for every 1,000 square feet of floor space occupied. It has been agreed with employee representatives that this staffing policy would continue.
Sales commission:	Based on the VAT-exclusive selling price at ten per cent. Of this amount one-half was paid directly to the relevant section head with the remainder being shared by the employees of that section.

Based on a casual analysis of the above costs, Allan realised that for planning and control purposes, costs of goods purchased and sales commission were the only costs considered to be truly variable in relation to sales activity. 'That should simplify my calculations considerably,' he thought to himself.

However the issue of adding a clothing boutique to the department store remained unresolved largely due to lack of financial analysis. Its addition would certainly draw a new type of clientele but there was always the possibility of lost revenue in the other clothing sections. The anticipated mark-up on cost on items in the boutique was not as good as existing items; Allan reckoned only fifty per cent on cost. However if he could manage to take 1,000 square feet from the household goods section Allan was confident that the boutique proposal was feasible. Nevertheless to be on the safe side he felt it would be necessary to spend an additional £10,000 on advertising in order to promote it.

REQUIREMENT

1 Prepare a statement for the year ending 31 December 1987 showing section contribution and the total profit of the store. Explain your workings. What level of sales would be required in 1988 to generate the same amount of profit as in the previous year?

2 Using your calculations in (1) comment on the relative profitability of each section assuming that limitations on floor space constrain the range of goods displayed and sold. Explain your conclusions.

3 What level of boutique sales would be necessary in the first year to make the proposal viable, assuming sales in all other sections declined by ten per cent? Explain your assumptions.

4 What changes and issues should be considered by Peter Allan? Specify your assumptions (if any).

Case 1.3 The Beta Company

Dave Barry, an electrical engineer, is the manager of the Beta Company which manufactures special electrical components to order. He took up his present position some years ago after obtaining an MBA degree. The company has been relatively profitable in recent years although sales, in volume terms, have shown little increase. He has recently been approached by a potentially new customer to produce a special component. Barry is unsure if the proposal would enable him to make any money on the project. One of his problems is that his firm's weekly production overhead has fluctuated widely in recent weeks. These fluctuations have made it difficult to estimate the level of production overhead that will be incurred for any single week.

The proposal which Barry is considering is for the production of 5,000 electrical components which can be produced using the firm's existing highly skilled labour force and machine-time capabilities. Each electrical component would require an input of one direct labour hour and ten minutes of machine time. Since the company is already operating at near capacity Barry realises that the necessary work would have to be performed on an overtime basis. Workers in such circumstances are paid at time-and-a-half.

Barry estimates that, on an overtime basis, the entire job would take about twelve weeks to complete and should be finished by mid December. The production manager and shop steward are enthusiastic about the proposal since it would boost employees' earnings prior to the Christmas holidays. Currently production workers are paid £6 per hour which provides them with gross earnings of about £200 per week. However taxes and social insurance deductions result in take home pay of about £160. For his part Barry sees the distinct possibility of purchasing additional plant and equipment next year if this special order situation translates itself into a regular and frequent commitment to purchase by the customer. After all the current price offer of £50 per unit represents an initial contract of £250,000. That kind of money should not be frowned upon, rather it should be encouraged.

From a costing point of view, the estimating department provided an analysis of raw materials required. Each unit produced requires three different types of raw materials designated A, B and C. The table on page 12 shows quantities required and additional information.

Material A is used regularly by the company in the production of other electrical components. However, material B is in excess of the company's requirements and unless used in the production of these units would have to be sold. The required amount of material C, since none are in stock, would be specially purchased.

However, the estimating department were reluctant to provide even

11

Raw material parts	Parts required per unit	Current stock level (parts)	Historic cost	Replacement cost	Net realisable value
A	1	5,000	£2	£4	£1
B	½	9,000	£3	£5	£2
C	2	nil	nil	£6	nil

'guesstimates' of production overheads which could be attributed to this job. The sales manager of the firm, Jack Russell, argued that they were irrelevant for pricing purposes because, by definition, they couldn't be attributed to an individual product. He argued that if only direct labour and materials were included in the costing it would enable a very competitive contract price to be quoted. A keen price would virtually guarantee the contract this time — profits could then be generated on subsequent business. If overheads were included in the quotation the company could end up pricing itself out of the market, and not just in the short term.

Dave Barry is not convinced by the argument of the 'irrelevancy' of production overheads in such circumstances. Rather he believes that an accurate classification of overheads is essential in both planning and controlling the operations of the firm. The first thing he must do is relate production overheads to some type of activity within the firm. However, he is unsure whether to use direct labour hours or machine hours as the best measure of activity. Ultimately a choice must be made between these two bases in order to determine a cost behaviour pattern. A trade association publication to which he subscribes indicates that, for companies manufacturing electrical components, overheads tend to vary with direct labour hours. On the other hand he realises that in his company a large portion of production overheads represent depreciation of factory equipment and energy costs which were calculated on a usage, i.e. hourly basis. The place to start, Dave reasons, is with an analysis of historical data.

The following data on total production overheads, direct labour hours and machine hours for the most recent twelve week period are collected (Exhibit 1) and Barry notes that they showed sufficient variability in activity levels to provide a useful start for prediction purposes.

Barry is confident that the above observations are representative of the current production process and that the relationships will be valid for the forthcoming period. There has not been any significant technological change in the production process in recent times and none was anticipated. His own informal work study calculations suggest that there is no experience or learning curve phenomenon in the production process. Certainly no significant standard cost variances relating to labour efficiency have appeared on the monthly production report.

Exhibit 1. Production overheads incurred and operating levels of activity

Week	Direct labour hours	Machine hours	Total production overheads
1	1,250	111	£29,900
2	1,497	132	34,600
3	1,184	121	28,900
4	1,499	147	34,300
5	1,356	154	32,400
6	1,300	125	31,200
7	1,222	122	28,700
8	1,259	131	29,400
9	1,109	120	27,000
10	1,435	144	33,400
11	1,121	112	27,700
12	1,433	145	34,100

General or specific price changes in relation to overheads during the past few months have been insignificant and no price changes are anticipated in the immediate future.

Having quickly revised a basic management accounting text dealing with cost prediction, Barry understands the various methods proposed for determining a cost behaviour pattern. These methods included the scatter diagram method, the high-low method and simple linear regression. He is unable to make up his mind on the best method to use since each has its own advantages and disadvantages. Perhaps he should use all three? But he realises that each would probably provide a different figure and he would be virtually back where he started!

REQUIREMENT

1 Determine the historical cost behaviour pattern of the production overhead costs using the scatter diagram method, the high-low method and simple linear regression. Justify your choice of independent, i.e. explanatory, variable.

2 Of the three proposed methods, which one should Barry use to determine the historical cost behaviour pattern of production overhead? Explain your choice indicating the reasons why the other methods are less desirable. Include reference to various criteria which can be used in choosing between alternative cost prediction models.

3 Would you recommend that Barry accept the proposal? How did you arrive at your conclusion? Would your recommendation change if the company was operating at considerably below maximum capacity?

4   Assume the following results were obtained from two simple linear regressions:

Simple regression analysis: results ($y = a + bx$)

	Regression No. 1	Regression No. 2
Dependent variable (y):	Production overhead costs	Production overhead costs
Independent variable (x):	Direct labour hours	Machine hours
Computed values:		
y-intercept	£5,520	£11,680
Coefficient of independent variable	19.49	147.96
Coefficient of correlation (R)	0.99	0.77
Standard error of estimate	448	1800
Standard error of regression coefficient for the independent variable	0.98	38.00
Coefficient of determination (R^2)	0.97	0.60
No. of observations	12	12
t-statistic required for a ninety-five per cent confidence interval:		
12 degrees of freedom	2.179	1.179
10 degrees of freedom	2.228	2.228

(a) Apply two tests to assess the linearity of both regressions. Which regression would you recommend to use? Why?

(b) Calculate a ninety-five per cent confidence interval for the variable production overhead per unit based on your preferred regression equation. To what extent could this confidence interval influence your recommendation of accepting or rejecting the order? Explain.

14

Case 1.4 The Maradona Manufacturing Company

The Maradona Manufacturing Company is a small manufacturing business which specialises in producing electrical devices that incorporate advanced technological features. The company has just received an order from a potential new customer for 128 identical devices which can be completed using Maradona's own labour-force and manufacturing capacity. The managing director, Peter Reid, called a head of department meeting to discuss the proposal.

THE MEETING

Peter Reid (Managing Director):

'Gentlemen, I would like to discuss with you a proposal to produce 128 special electronic devices received from X-Tel Ltd, with whom we have not previously traded. We have already incurred £1,000 by way of entertaining X-Tel personnel so we have already committed ourselves to some extent. The order represents about twenty per cent of our current monthly output and I understand we currently have the spare machine capacity to deal with it. However, there may be some problems with labour. Perhaps Sean would fill us in on the main technical details?'

Sean Murray is the production manager. He explains that initially these components will undergo normal operations in the assembly department. For each unit all the necessary material parts are issued at the start of the process and are gradually assembled by skilled workers. The production cost figures, he explains, should be identical with the normal production operations. Last month's production and cost summary appears in Exhibit 1.

Exhibit 1. Monthly production and cost summary

Opening work in progress	nil
Units started	600
Units completed and transferred to finishing process	400
Closing work in progress	200
(one-fifth complete as to conversion costs)	
Basic material parts issued to assembly during month	£60,000
Conversion costs incurred during month	£22,000

Conversion costs represent assembly labour. However, Maradona could only produce these special components by working overtime at time-and-a-half, since assembly labour is currently at full stretch and will be so for the foreseeable future. Once the units are assembled they are transferred for finishing.

Barry Davis is acting head of the finishing department. He indicates that the finishing process is very simple for these special devices, since only two components, namely Alpha and Beta, need to be added. The relevant data on quantities required of Alpha and Beta are:

Component	Units required per device	Current stock (units)	Historic cost	Current replacement cost	Net realisable value
Alpha	2	300	£3	£4	£2
Beta	1	100	£2	£3	£1

Component Alpha is used regularly and continuously in the finishing department in the normal manufacturing operations whereas Beta components have been left over from an order completed some months previously. They are surplus to requirements and the company has no planned use for them. However they have a small net realisable value in the sense that they could be sold to other manufacturers.

Davis points out that it is important not to overlook the shortage of labour in the finishing department. Finishing labour is currently paid £6 per hour and 4 hours is required per unit of special component. However to accept this special order all necessary finishing labour would have to be transferred from existing work and these orders would consequently be lost. He stresses that in accepting this special order the company is incurring an opportunity cost. At the moment the necessary finishing labour are working on a job which yield a unit surplus as follows:

Existing work in finishing department (per unit)

Sales price		£25
Finishing labour	£12	
Materials	9	21
		4

The discussion then centers on the costs of packaging these special components. The purchasing manager, John Moore confirms that packaging costs would be the same as the current units produced and consist mainly of cardboard boxes with one box required per finished unit. He explains that the company already has standing delivery for 650 boxes per month. The supplier charges £2 per box but would reduce the price by five per cent on all units for any orders over 700 units. John Moore is unsure what to do about ordering additional packaging materials but at the same time appreciates that the quantity discount could be attractive.

Gary Stephens, the firm's accountant explains that there are a few other cost items which may be relevant to the discussion. Firstly, the firm operates a monthly flexible budget formula in relation to planning and controlling production overheads. The flexible budget formula is:

16

Total monthly production overheads are £10,000 + 0.5 DLH (where DLH represents total hours worked in the finishing department only). The company uses the direct labour hours in the finishing department only for convenience but Stephens confirms that the formula had been fairly accurate in recent times.

Secondly, sales commission is payable at the rate of five per cent of quotation price on all orders. There is some discussion as to whether commission should be payable in respect of special orders such as this since the proposal did not originate through the efforts of the sales personnel. Eventually the meeting's participants agree that it should be taken into consideration since there were a number of precedents. Finally, there is the question of quality control. Since all of the work is to be done on the overtime basis the firm would need to provide for an additional supervisor for three months until the job is finished. The current salary for a supervisor is £12,000 per annum. However, Jack Doyle, who has just retired as a supervisor on a pension of £5,000 per annum payable by the company agrees to stay on if required and waive his pension for the period.

Lunch time being imminent, Peter Reid intervenes; 'I think we should adjourn the meeting for lunch and meanwhile Gary can prepare a bid based on relevant costs. We normally add a thirty per cent mark-up on cost to determine quotation price, so Gary, please let us have your thoughts on that!'

REQUIREMENT

1   Prepare an estimate of the minimum quotation price that Gary Stephens would recommend to charge for the proposed contract. Your answer should be in the nature of a cost schedule clearly indicating the individual cost items.

2   Briefly suggest other factors which would be taken into consideration before a final decision on quotation price is taken.

Case 1.5 Kent Manufacturing Company

In January 1986, Robert Baxter organised a meeting of his staff to discuss product policy decisions in the Kent Manufacturing Company. Baxter was managing director of the company and as such was fully responsible for the profit performance of his modern manufacturing plant which produces sensor and analyser boards for security systems.

Reports from sales representatives indicated that the forthcoming year would be one of sales decline for the company's products. If accurate, such assessments would mean that the company would be operating significantly below 100 per cent capacity but nevertheless above break-even point. If necessary, production and assembly labour would operate on a two or three day working week due to shortage of orders.

Faced with the prospect of idle-production capacity for the forthcoming year, Baxter was anxious to acquire new customers even if it meant adapting existing products to market needs or even producing totally new products. One large, potential customer was identified and Kent had recently been asked to tender for the production of special sensor boards, which represented a slight adaptation to one of the company's main products. In this context Baxter called a meeting of the various department managers.

THE MEETING

Robert Baxter (Managing director):

'Gentlemen, our current sales forecasts indicate a significant amount of idle production capacity in our plant next year. We more or less anticipated this at our last meeting. I think we should try to utilise this spare capacity to tender for special contract work since this is a realistic way to improve our profits. The job I want to specifically consider here is the proposal to tender for the production of 10,240 special sensor boards. Dan, perhaps you could fill us in?'

Dan Sullivan (Production manager):

'Perhaps I should first fill you in on the main technical details. This special sensor board can be manufactured fairly easily in two separate in-house departments. In department A the materials, represented mainly by various electrical components, would be issued at the beginning of the process and gradually assembled and soldered to the sensor board. The work is fairly routine and our workers are well trained in this technique. We have the spare capacity and I don't anticipate any problem in this area. If we get this contract we can keep on the workers rather than letting them go on a two-day week.

In department B the board is coated basically with a special heat

18

resisting substance and has to be specially tested before being allocated to finished stock. However the official specification for this job has requested a specific heat resisting substance that we don't normally use and that's going to add twenty per cent to our normal conversion costs in this department. As Tom shall explain to you, these conversion costs mainly include labour.'

Tom Lee (Accountant):
'Our cost accounting system allocates raw materials and conversion costs directly to the departments in question on a usage basis. We don't allocate any overheads to the departments. Rather we determine an approximate overhead absorption rate for the entire production process at the start of the year and use it consistently for pricing purposes. As a matter of policy we have always considered that full cost pricing is the major determinant of profit. After all if prices don't cover costs we can't make a profit. If we don't make a profit we don't stay in business.'

Robert Baxter (Managing director):
'Wait a minute Tom! This is a special order situation and I'm anxious to quote the cheapest price possible. We mightn't make a lot of money on the contract but at least the lads won't have to go on short time and we get a new customer.'

Tom Lee (Accountant):
'I accept your point but the immediate problem is that we don't have calculations on the actual overhead costs. Indeed the only data I have is that relating to units produced and total relevant overheads incurred in both departments over the past year (Exhibit 1).

Exhibit 1. Production overheads and units produced per month

	Units produced	Overheads (Depts A and B)
Jan	18,000	£270,000
Feb	18,000	210,000
Mar	15,000	195,000
April	15,000	225,000
May	12,000	195,000
June	12,000	180,000
July	9,000	150,000
Aug	9,000	135,000
Sept	6,000	90,000
Oct	6,000	135,000
Nov	3,000	90,000
Dec	3,000	105,000
	126,000	1,980,000

What I shall have to do is work out an overhead rate per unit. As you probably know the theory of overhead allocation and absorption is not one of the accountancy profession's proudest achievements! I'll use regression analysis since it is probably the best way to measure the relationship between two variables.'

Robert Baxter (Managing director):
'That information would be very useful, Tom. It might be as well to give us information on material and conversion costs. Don't forget to add twenty per cent to your calculations for conversion costs in Department B — we don't want to underprice. By the way, what should we do about the proposed ten per cent increase in the price of basic raw materials? We have a lot in stock at the old price but yet we use these materials regularly.'

(Tom Lee looked at the latest Departmental Production and Cost Report [Exhibit 2] and realised he must brush up on his process and relevant cost accounting.)

Baxter (continued):
'Is there anything else that we should specifically consider about this proposal?'

Jack Kelly (Assistant production manager):
'There are two features we haven't discussed yet. According to the tender specification these sensor boards must be packaged in an unusual way — I think the units are being exported intact — and shall need extra reinforcers, four per box. In addition basic packaging materials cost £1 per box and ten sensor boards must be packed in each box. So we need to specially train one of our packing work force. We have done a few trial runs on time taken and believe that the first box of ten sensor boards can be packaged in fifty minutes. The really interesting thing is that we believe that the more experience the employee has in packaging this box the less time it will take to perform the task. This phenomenon is referred to as the learning curve and we realistically estimate a twenty per cent learning rate. In simple language this means that as output doubles the average time for all boxes packaged will be eighty per cent of the previous average time. This factor could be a significant cost saving especially since packing labour is paid £10 per hour. The person I have in mind to do the job is young Smith who would otherwise be let go due to lack of orders.'

James Long (Sales manager):
'Sorry to interrupt at this stage but we agreed at a meeting some time ago that a sales commission of five per cent of sales/quotation price on all special orders be paid. I think that policy should be adhered to!

20

In addition we normally add ten per cent to all our cost estimates to give us a satisfactory mark-up.'

Robert Baxter (Managing Director):
'Point taken, James. Commission should be included in our cost calculations but I don't know about a mark-up. I think we should adjourn the meeting until tomorrow morning to give us time to think things over. Meanwhile Tom can you produce a minimum cost quotation as a basis for further discussion?'

Exhibit 2. Departmental Production and Cost Report (December, 1987)

| | Department | |
	A	B
Production data		
Work in progress, 1 December:		
Department A	nil	nil
Department B (100 per cent complete as to prior department costs; 25 per cent complete as to conversion costs).	—	800
New units started	6,000	—
Units received from Department A		4,000
Units completed and transferred to Department B	4,000	—
Finished goods (from Department B)	—	3,000
Work in progress, 31 December:		
Department A (100 per cent complete as to material costs; 20 per cent complete as to conversion costs)	2,000	—
Department B (100 per cent complete as to prior department costs; one-third complete as to conversion costs)	—	1,800
Cost data		
Stock, 1 December		
Prior department costs	nil	£12,000
Conversion costs	nil	£6,000
Costs added this month		
Materials	£60,000	nil
Conversion costs	£22,000	£102,000

When the meeting concluded Tom Lee went back to his office and phoned his wife, 'Hello! Listen I'm sorry but I have to work late tonight. Baxter came on heavy this afternoon and I've got to do an urgent report for the morning ... Bye.'

REQUIREMENT

1 Prepare a 'minimum bid' quotation for the production of 10,240 special sensor boards. Explain your figures.

2 What issues have been overlooked in your calculations'.

NOTES

1 The normal equations for simple regression are:

$$Ey = a.N + b.Ex$$
$$Exy = a.Ex + b.Ex^2$$

where N = number of observations in sample.

Ey = the sum of values of the dependent variable.

a = parameter (constant) to be estimated.

b = parameter (coefficient) of the independent variable.

Ex = the sum of values of the independent variable.

$E(x^2)$ = the sum of the squared values of the independent variable.

Exy = the sum of the product of x times y

2 The learning process can be described by an exponential function of the following form:

$$y = a.X^b$$

where: y = the cumulative average amount of time taken to package X boxes.

a = the amount of time taken to package the first box.

X = total number of boxes to be packaged.

b = an index of learning, equal to the log of the learning rate divided by the log of 2.

Case 1.6 The Patriot Hotel

It was late September. Richard Delahunt sat at his desk surrounded by a vast amount of operating and financial data concerning his hotel and leisure complex. It was near the end of the summer season, a poor one by recent standards. Richard had to decide whether to close down operations as planned on 15 October or whether to keep all facilities open and running all year. It was important that he made his decision quickly. His staff would have to be notified and asked to extend their working season. In addition, Richard felt that he would have to notify patrons that, contrary to previous years, the facilities were available right through the winter months.

Richard Delahunt was the owner and general manager of the Patriot Hotel which was located in a medium-sized coastal town in the west of Ireland. After graduating in hotel management some years previously he took up employment in the hotel which was then jointly owned by his parents. His father retired shortly afterwards and Richard soon had to assume responsibility for all the major policy and operating decisions. To date his only major decision was to endorse the building of a small leisure complex in the grounds of the hotel. It was a costly venture, initially conceived by his father, but Richard had no doubt that this major development had boosted the hotel's turnover significantly in recent years.

The hotel itself has fifty bedrooms each with its own bathroom and shower unit. There is also a ballroom which doubles as a function room, a restaurant which is renowned for its culinary standard and elegance, a bar and the leisure centre. The leisure centre consists of two squash courts, a twenty metre indoor heated swimming pool and a sauna bath. These leisure facilities are available free to hotel patrons. All other users either pay a six-monthly family membership in advance or pay on a usage basis.

It was traditional that all facilities in the 'Patriot' opened on 15 April for a six month period, generously described in Ireland as the 'summer season'. The appalling bad weather during the recent summer and the decline in foreign tourists to the region had hit badly this season's trade. The much heralded VAT reductions on hotels and restaurants had little impact on sales even though the reductions were genuinely passed on by the hotel to its patrons. It appeared that customers were not very price sensitive. With ever increasing running costs and interest payments on recent borrowings Richard realised that the hotel would find it difficult to remain profitable in future years, especially if sales could not be significantly expanded beyond their current level. It was in this context that he was contemplating making all facilities available to patrons the year round. It was an ambitious thought but the most important consideration was whether it would be prudent to do so. Richard knew that his proposal would have to be commercial and very serious thought should be given to the various cost and revenue elements in the financial planning process.

The anticipated results for the six months ending 15 October, which was only three weeks away, are provided in Exhibit 1.

Exhibit 1. Operating statement for six months ending 15 October 1987 (180 days)

	Hotel	Restaurant and bar	Leisure complex	Total
Sales	£113,400	£40,500	£27,000	£180,900
Cost of sales	8,100	12,150	—	20,250
Light and heat	14,300	2,100	2,400	18,800
Salaries	43,600	16,000	10,600	70,200
Insurance, rates and security	12,300	1,600	3,300	17,200
Cleaning	16,200	2,000	2,700	20,900
Administration and financing etc.	17,000	6,000	4,600	27,600
Net profit	1,900	650	3,400	5,950

There were a number of difficult assumptions to be made in order to evaluate the financial impact of staying open during the winter season. The most important variable, Richard had remembered from his hotel management studies, was room occupancy. Average room lettings in the hotel during the summer season represented a constant ninety per cent capacity. However for the winter months the best that could be anticipated was a forty per cent occupancy rate provided the rate charged per room was reduced by £5 per day. It was company policy to charge a fixed price per room regardless of the number of occupants. Thus the occupant of a single room was charged the same price as a room with two or three occupants.

Delahunt estimated that one-half of the restaurant and bar sales were attributable directly to room occupancy rates and this relationship would hold valid during the winter months. The remaining sales of the restaurant and bar were attributed to non-residents, mainly locals. Richard reckoned that such sales to non-residents could be maintained at a similar volume for the next six months. As an added attraction Richard decided that he would hire a pianist to play in the foyer of the hotel on Friday and Saturday evenings for a nightly fee of £25. In addition no restaurant price increases were anticipated for the winter season.

Forecasting potential sales revenue for the leisure centre was more

24

problematic. Two-thirds of current revenue during the summer months was in the nature of family membership whereby a fixed fee was paid at the start of the season. This entitled any family member to unrestricted and free use of the facilities up to 15 October. Since all family membership was virtually confined to local inhabitants, Richard was sure that ninety per cent of families would extend their membership for the winter months on payment of a similar sum. Indeed many family members had specifically requested an extended season. The remaining revenue of the leisure centre during the summer months was generated mainly from tourists and casual visitors to the locality. At best Richard anticipated that only twenty per cent of such revenue would be generated during the winter months.

In order to evaluate the financial impact of extending the operating season, Richard rearranged the cost data from the operating statement such that it indicated both the fixed and variable components of the various costs incurred (Exhibit 2). Richard believed that his cost analysis was a useful basis on which to produce preliminary cost estimates for the winter months. After all he estimated to be closed only over the short Christmas period, giving a 180 day working season.

Exhibit 2. Analysis of costs for six months ending 15 October 1987

Fixed costs:	Hotel	Restaurant	Leisure centre	Total
Salaries (6 months)	£43,600	£16,000	£10,600	£70,200
Light and heat (annual charge)	5,000	1,000	1,000	7,000
Insurance, rates and security (annual charge)	12,300	1,600	3,300	17,200
Cleaning wages (6 months)	4,000	1,000	1,000	6,000
Administration and financing (annual charge)	17,000	6,000	4,600	27,600
Variable costs:				
Cost of sales	8,100	12,150	—	20,250
Light and heat	9,300	1,100	1,400	11,800
Cleaning	12,200	1,000	1,700	14,900

His analysis confirmed that some of his operating costs were fixed in that they were incurred regardless of the level of activity and covered a twelve-month rather than a six-month period.

The biggest cost element of the hotel was salaries and if he wished to remain open during the winter months he must first extend all the employees' contracts. Everyone would be asked to stay and he believed everyone would. This announcement would boost staff morale and automatically eliminate the bother of recruiting staff at the start of the summer season next year. As things stood good quality staff were reluctant to join the hotel for the summer season since the period of employment was limited to six months.

Light and heating costs would be more difficult to predict. He estimated that in the hotel they would fluctuate with room occupancy rates. In the restaurant and bar they would be about twenty per cent higher than in the summer, whereas in the leisure complex they would double during the winter. Variable cleaning costs would remain at the same percentage of occupancy/usage as at present since they were largely incurred as a result of usage of facilities.

Richard appreciated that his preliminary cost analysis was a little unscientific and imperfect. Nevertheless he was confident that he could get a fairly good picture as to whether it was financially worthwhile to extend the hotel's operating season or not. His eventual goal was a profit level of at least £5,000 for opening during the winter season. However, his immediate concern was the liquidity position of the business since the hotel did not have a large surplus of cash and the bank would be reluctant to grant additional loan facilities. As a result Delahunt wanted to know what volume of sales would have to be generated over the winter months in order to cover the additional, expected cash outflows.

REQUIREMENT

1   Identify the financial impact of the proposed six month's extension to the hotel's operating season based on Richard's assumptions.

2   Explain what you consider to be the critical factors and assumptions (financial and non-financial) underlying this decision.

3   At what level of sales will the proposed extension over the winter months break-even? Generate a profit of £5,000? Explain your calculations.

Case 1.7 Wholesome Foods Limited

Wholesome Foods Limited has recently engaged in the processing of soya beans for the Irish market. The managing director of the company, Jack Cullen, was attracted to the proposal some months ago. His firm already produced an extensive range of health food products which were sold to retailers around the country under the brand name of 'Wholesome Foods'. Market research indicated to Cullen that his brand was the market leader in the country. This was good news. However, the research also revealed a small but rapidly expanding demand for both soya bean oil and soya bean meal, which apparently were being supplied to the same retailers by a small independent processer. Cullen felt that soya bean products would be an ideal and logical addition to his health food range and quickly decided to take on this competition.

Cullen's soya bean processing operation was carried out in a specially rented premises adjacent to the main manufacturing operations of the company. Because of space restrictions in his main factory this arrangement was expected to continue in the forseeable future. The soya bean processing operation itself was fairly simple. The basic raw material ingredients were imported from abroad. Initially the raw materials were cleaned and subsequently roasted. The beans were then ground through a press while liquids were simultaneously added, mixed and heated. The end result was separate outputs of soya bean oil and a powdered residue or cake. The oil was then cooled and immediately bottled, packaged and sold to retailers in one litre bottles at £1 per bottle. Thus the company incurred no selling expenses on this product.

Next the powdered residue was transferred to a separating process since the residue could not be sold without further processing. This process involves mixing the powdered residue with additional ingredients so as to form soya bean meal. Due to the ingredients added during the separating process the powdered residue had a normal weight gain of ten per cent. The output of the separating process was then sifted several times and ninety per cent of the ultimate output represented soya bean meal which was then bagged and sold to retailers at a price of £2.30 per kilogram. However the separating process always resulted in a very small, solid waste which was not fit for human consumption and had no market value. Referred to as 'thrash' it typically represented ten-per cent of the output of the separating process. The company had made arrangements with a waste disposal firm to dump this waste on a regular basis at a weekly cost of £25. The processing operation is depicted in Figure 1.

Wholesome Foods Ltd had been extremely busy during the past few months since the demand for all their products had exceeded expectations. At last Cullen thought, the Irish public were becoming

Figure 1. Processing of soya beans

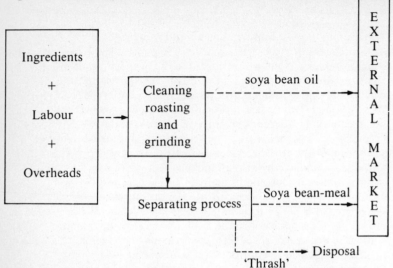

more conscious of health foods. The health slogan 'You are what you eat' was gaining acceptance and impetus. However one unfortunate result of this frenetic activity was that the firm's accounting system was not up-to-date. Sitting in his office in the quiet of a late Friday evening Cullen resolved to update himself on his soya bean operations. He wondered whether his initial venture into soya bean processing had been profitable. At least 900 litres of oil had been sold during the last quarter in addition to 9,000 kilograms of meal.

Working late into the evening Cullen eventually isolated all the financial and operating data regarding soya bean processing which had commenced only thirteen weeks ago. The company initially purchased twelve tons of soya beans at a cost of £100 per ton, of which ten tons had been processed during the period. Other joint costs of the cleaning and grinding process were:

Direct labour	£6,000
Variable production overhead	2,000
Rent and insurance	1,000
Share of administration costs	2,000

The cleaning and separating process yielded 1,000 litres of soya bean oil and 10,000 kilograms of powdered residue. The oil was bottled, labled and packaged at a cost of 3p per litre.

28

The costs assigned to the separating process were:

Direct labour	£3,000
Variable production overhead	1,000
Rent and insurance	1,000

In addition, packaging costs for the meal amounted to 4p per kilogram.

Apart from estimating the overall profitability of his soya bean processing operation, Cullen was contemplating the possibility of further processing 'thrash' into a genuine animal feed supplement. The idea had been put to him some time ago by a veterinary surgeon who was a personal friend and with whom he played a round of golf on a regular basis.

His friend Michael, the vet, explained, 'You can take this "thrash" and mix it with several other ingredients, mainly mineral supplements, to produce a very good animal feed. If it's available, farmers will buy it since an animal won't thrive during the winter months on silage alone. Farmers now recognise the importance of winter feed supplements for their cattle. Even horse breeders would be interested in purchasing.'

Cullen realised that this product offered a promising means of disposing of all his 'thrash' output in the future. He commissioned market research, at a cost of £1,000, to investigate the sales potential among local farmers and horse breeders. This research revealed a demand for his animal feed supplement if it was available in 5 kilogram packs and provided it was competitively priced. Cullen interpreted his finding as allowing a selling price of £14 per bag. Additional ingredients, including mineral supplements, necessary for the animal feed would amount to £10 per pack and variable packaging costs were estimated at 10p per pack. In addition, special mixing equipment would have to be rented at a monthly cost of £200. However mixing operations would be performed by the existing labour force. At first sight the proposal to further process 'thrash' certainly seemed a good idea. But was it worthwhile, Cullen thought to himself?

REQUIREMENT

1 Prepare calculations to indicate whether the soya bean oil and soya bean meal processing operation was profitable or otherwise during the past quarter. Include a joint cost allocation for closing stock valuation purposes. Explain and defend your calculations.

2 If the powdered residue could be sold immediately at split-off point (without further processing) for £15,000, would you recommend immediate sale or further processing? Why?

3 Calculate the minimum number of five-kilogram packs of animal feed supplement that would have to be sold per quarter in order to justify their manufacture. (You should assume that all 'thrash' would be further processed and any unsold packs would be given away free of charge).

29

Case 1.8 Merrion Products Limited

Merrion Products Limited was incorporated and commenced trading in 1979. Its several shareholders consisted of members of the Carroll family. The business was devoted to the import of a raw material substance which was slightly refined for Irish tastes and sold to customers around the country. During the initial years of production, product 'A' was the only product manufactured and the profits were adequate to satisfy the family shareholders. During the 1980s it was decided to introduce new products based on the same raw material but refined in different ways. In 1981, product 'B' was introduced and product 'C' was added the following year. Both products were an immediate success and the entire production output for both products was sold by the end of the year. In fact demand for all products constantly outstripped production. Encouraged by this success, product 'D', based on the same raw material was introduced into the product range last year after extensive research on customers' tastes. It was considered by all family members to be as equally successful as the other three products.

According to the audited financial statements Merrion Products Limited was a profitable company with excellent cash flow. The various family members concentrated mainly on the administrative and selling side of the business. Each family member was entitled to a basic salary which was supplemented by a share of total sales commission. The sales commission was calculated at the rate of ten per cent of sales price on every unit sold. Thus each family member would participate in the overall success of his firm. The Carroll family believed that the company's profitability was mainly attributable to two factors. First, was the high quality of its products with guaranteed delivery dates. Michael Carroll, the managing director of the firm, often boasted that the number of customer complaints in any one year could be counted on the fingers of one hand. The second reason was due to subtle marketing and presentation so that each product was perceived by the public as different and was sold to different types of customer. In other words the products were not considered complementary and had their own unique brand loyalty. Thus the demand for one product could fluctuate without affecting the sales of the other products, or the refusal of orders for one product would not lead to cancellation of orders for the others.

Each product was produced from the same basic raw material which was imported from abroad. Until recently this raw material had been available in unlimited quantities and purchased by Merrion quarterly in advance as required. However recent political instability in the exporting country resulted in a severe restriction on the availability of this raw material. A recent fact-finding visit to the exporting country only served to confirm the restricted availability of the imported raw material in the forthcoming year. On his return home Michael Carroll called a directors' meeting to discuss the problem and its impact on the budget for the forthcoming quarter.

Una Carroll, the only daughter in the family, was company accountant. After obtaining a business studies degree at college she immediately joined the family firm. Mainly concerned with maintaining the basic financial accounting records and keeping control over accounts receivable and payable, she also monitored progress towards agreed budget targets. However the budget setting process for each quarter was unsophisticated in that output levels were determined by amicable consensus amongst family members. Preference was usually given to the highest-priced item since this procedure maximised sales commission for the family members. Una tried to pursuade the other members of the family that there was a more scientific method available to determine best production plans. However whenever she mentioned the phrase 'profit maximisation' in discussion her family always retorted, 'But that's only theory Una, and has nothing got to do with practice.' Being the youngest in the family Una felt she lacked a great deal of authority and credibility.

The Carroll family felt that the business did not need a management accountant since they considered the overall operations to be fairly simple. Neither did they require the services of a production manager or a marketing manager since they could virtually sell everything they produced. Una knew from experience that as long as budgeted profit was higher than last year then everyone was happy. Generally, the actual financial performance met the budget targets pretty well.

At the start of the meeting Michael Carroll relayed to participants details of his foreign trip. He explained,

'Unfortunately our worst suspicions have been confirmed. I saw things at first hand and also had discussions with our embassy officials. I made direct contact with our usual supplier and he indicated that he will be unable to deliver more than £72,000 of raw materials per quarter until conditions improve and that's unlikely to be for some time. The basic problem, he tells me is that the material is simply not available in his country due to the current political situation. Since my return home I have made extensive enquiries regarding possible alternative suppliers of the same raw material in other countries. There just isn't any which we could tap at this short notice. Like many simple problems, its insoluble in the short-term. We've just got to accept it from now!'

Una interrupted, 'I expect that our budgets for the next quarter shall have to be revised — downwards — and our profits shall be considerably depressed as a result.' She circulated the previously agreed budget and supporting schedules for the forthcoming quarter to participants (Exhibits 1 and 2).

Una continued, 'In my opinion there is no scope for any reduction in costs. We can't change, at least in the short-term, our direct material costs neither can we change our packaging costs. Our direct labour consists of the part-time assembly workers which we need in order to produce. Likewise variable overheads will be incurred if we want to produce, and our fixed overheads are already down to an absolute minimum. Commission is the only thing that we could effectively cut.'

Michael Carroll interjected, 'No, I recommend that the sales commission be left alone. We're all in this venture together and I reckon we're going to have to sell our way out of our problems. We need to retain the incentive to sell and keep our selling prices intact.'

Everyone agreed.

Exhibit 1. Budget for the quarter ending 31 March 1988

Budget sales		£200,000
Cost of production		149,500
Gross margin		50,500
Administration expenses	£19,900	
Distribution expenses	5,700	
Sales commission	20,000	
Financial expenses	800	46,400
Budget net profit		4,100

Exhibit 2. Schedule of revenue and production costs per product

Product	A	B	C	D
Sales price	£20	£40	£30	£20
Direct material (imported)	7	16	13	10
Direct labour and packing	3	4	6	4
Production overhead	4	5	6	5
Budget sales (units)	1,500	2,000	2,000	1,500

NOTE: Production overhead includes both fixed and variable expense. The estimated fixed overhead for the forthcoming quarter amounts to £20,000 and has been apportioned to each product on the basis of total anticipated sales revenue of each product.

Patrick Carroll, the eldest member of the family, who was chiefly responsible for sales, raised the possibility of maximum sales levels of each product. He said, 'We must take into consideration that there is a definite limit on the amount of goods which we can sell at existing prices next quarter.'

Michael Carroll accepted that the point was valid. After much discussion all family members agreed that maximum sales revenue of each product at current prices for the forthcoming quarter would be as follows:

Product A	£60,000
Product B	88,000
Product C	63,000
Product D	40,000

Subsequently everyone at the meeting realised that due to the definite shortage of raw materials it was not possible to produce simultaneously all these quantities. Michael Carroll added, 'I think we shall have to be more selective in what we produce in future. However, I recommend that we produce a minimum of 1,000 units of each product during the forthcoming quarter. This would, at least, keep the company's products in the minds of the public and satisfy our major customers. It is important to do this. Any remaining materials should be used in the most profitable manner. Una, now is the ideal time to put some of that theory of yours into practice. If you feel that there is a single, best way to utilise our production facilities in these circumstances now is the time to let us know.'

REQUIREMENT

1   Prepare a statement showing the most profitable production plan for Merrion Products Ltd for the forthcoming quarter. Prepare a detailed profit and loss account to accompany your recommendation. Explain your workings.

2   Calculate the firm's break-even point for the forthcoming quarter. What fundamental assumptions have you made?

3   What is the 'opportunity cost', if any, associated with the minimum production of 1,000 units of each product?

4   Assuming it was possible to increase all selling prices by £7 per unit without influencing demand, would this price increase effect your analysis? Explain.

Case 1.9 Morello Manufacturing Company*

You have recently been appointed to the newly-created position of management accountant in the Morello Manufacturing Company. The company is owned by Mr Joe Smith who occupies the position of managing director. He is an engineer by profession and has just been awarded an MBA degree from the local university. Until recently production and sales quota decisions have been made exclusively by Smith, without consulting department heads, on the basis of intuition and a certain degree of inspiration. In spite of this unusual and frequently autocratic style of management, the company has been reasonably profitable.

While studying for his MBA, Smith gradually realised that the company's current information system and decision-making process could and should be significantly improved. His first step in this regard was your appointment as management accountant which was quickly followed by a short memorandum to department heads requesting them to 'prepare' for a heads of department meeting at which a budget for the forthcoming year would be discussed.

To generate preliminary discussion Mr Ball, the financial accountant, circulated a summarised profit and loss account for the first ten months of the current year (Exhibit 1). Ball is a quiet man who seems to spend much of his time trying to cope with the transition from a manual to a computerised accounting system. You have been told in confidence that he tends to agree with the suggestions made by the managing director in order to avoid any form of confrontation.

Exhibit 1. Profit and loss account for ten months ending October 1987

Sales revenue		£3,640,000
Less: Cost of sales		
Direct materials	£768,000	
Direct labour	865,500	
Production overheads	999,000	2,632,500
Gross margin		1,007,500
Selling and administrative expenses		924,000
Net profit		83,500

Mr Ball explained that the term 'production overhead' was used to describe a series of expenses incurred in the manufacture of the various products. This included some indirect labour and supervision, but mainly energy costs and maintenance and depreciation of plant and

---

*Participants should realise that the appropriate statistical techniques required in this case have already been performed and are contained in Exhibit 4.

equipment. It was clarified for the participants that selling and administrative expenses included sales commission payable at the rate of ten per
cent of sales price. Each product has its own sales force working on a
commission only basis. This arrangement was for taxation reasons since
each 'consultant' provided his own car and absorbed his own travelling
expenses. As a result each sales consultant would sell only that product
for which he is responsible.

While the participants of the meeting agreed that the profit performance of the firm was satisfactory, Smith suggested that such a
financial summary did not provide adequate information to facilitate
decision-making and budget preparation for the forthcoming year.
Smith complained; 'We don't even know our break-even point. Surely
there is more detailed information available on our various products
that could help us!'

Mr Ball responded that he had obtained some specific information
from the accounting records and produced the following table regarding
unit selling prices, sales units, production costs and other operating data
for each of the three products manufactured and sold by the firm
(Exhibit 2).

Exhibit 2.

	Alpha	Beta	Cappa
Selling price	£27.00	£25.00	£45.00
Direct materials	4.00	8.00	16.00
Direct labour	7.00	5.00	8.50
Variable overhead	7.70	5.50	9.35

Machine hours required per unit

	Alpha	Beta	Cappa
Assembly dept.	1 hour	0.5 hour	0.25 hour
Finishing dept.	0.5 hour	0.5 hour	1.25 hours

Analysis of sales revenue for the current period
Alpha: 90,000 units at £27 each = 2,430,000
Beta: 25,000 units at £25 each = 625,000
Cappa: 13,000 units at £45 each = 585,000
£3,640,000

One of the sales managers suggested that the first consideration to be
determined in the preparation of the next year's budget was minimum
production levels for each product. He argued that it was important for
the firm to satisfy the needs of valued customers, regardless of the cost
involved. After some discussion the following minimum production
quotas were agreed for the forthcoming year as:

Alpha 20,000 units
Beta 15,000 units
Cappa 10,000 units

Smith acknowledged the logic of this argument but asked, 'Can anyone tell me in simple language, how much it is costing us, in lost profits, to look after these customers?'

To end an uneasy silence Ball responded, 'It's difficult to know really.' Then changing the discussion, he added that at current prices, which were not expected to change, maximum sales of each product for the forthcoming year should also be considered. Looking realistically at the current performance and bearing in mind what the sales consultants were saying, maximum unit sales were agreed as follows:

Alpha   110,000 units
Beta   38,000 units
Cappa   20,000 units

The sales manager responsible for the Alpha product suggested that there was a large, unsatisfied demand for his product. He argued that the agreed sales limit of 110,000 units could easily be increased if it were made available through supermarkets. He indicated that one major supermarket chain would accept the product for one year on payment of £10,000 of 'hello' money. He added, 'I think such a move would be a good idea.'

Smith acknowledged the idea and then asked, 'Do we have any production capacity problems?'

The production manager said that the two main problems facing his departments in the forthcoming year were the shortage of raw materials and the limited avilability of machine hours. He explained that the availability of raw materials for the next year was limited to £1 million since the regular supplier was already overcommitted. It was not possible to arrange additional supplies at such short notice. He continued: 'The biggest problem we face is the shortage of machine capacity. Our machines have physical capacities of 120,000 and 100,000 hours per annum in the assembly and finishing departments respectively. The only way that we could permanently increase these facilities is to acquire highly specialised and expensive equipment and it would take well over a year before they would be operational. To make matters worse we would have to pay cash up front for them.'

Smith interrupted, 'any proposals for increased spending on equipment, advertising or anything else, would have to be carefully considered because of the weak cash flow position,' he said.

The production manager, Brian Gregory continued, 'Well there is an interesting short term possibility. We could purchase some second-hand machines for the finishing department at a forthcoming auction. I've seen them and we could have them installed and in good working order by the start of 1988. It would mean that both departments would have the same machine hour capacity.'

Two other possible solutions to the limited machine capacity problem were discussed. Initially price increases, in order to reduce product demand, were rejected due to their long term implications. It was acknowledged that price increases might boost short-term profits, but in the long-term customer goodwill would be adversely affected, especially since rival products existed and the products were considered to be price-sensitive. In many ways the company was a price-taker rather than a price-maker. Secondly Ball suggested that the firm could augment it's own production capacity in both departments by contractual agreements with independent manufacturers. 'At the present time,' he added, 'there are a few such contractors in the vicinity.'

Aware of the lack of progress and aware of the impending rush hour traffic, accentuated by a rock concert in the local football stadium, Mr Ball suggested, 'There is a simple way of tackling next year's budget.' He argued that since Beta had the lowest unit labour cost, all the remaining production capacity (after the minimum production quotas) should be directed entirely to the production of Beta. He produced the following projection supporting his argument (Exhibit 3) which indicated the utilisation of £1million worth of raw materials.

Exhibit 3. Proposed budget for 1988

Sales revenue:	Alpha	20,000 units at £8.30 each	£166,000
	Beta	95,000 units at £6.50 each	617,500
	Cappa	10,000 units at £11.15 each	111,500
Direct contribution			895,000
Less: Production overheads (say) 999,000			
Selling and administration (say) 924,000			1,923,000
Net loss projected			1,028,000

Mr Ball pointed out that this budget target for 1988 represented a significant deterioration on the actual results of the current period. He indicated that his figures were 'subject to revision' but was confident that they would not be significantly altered.

Brian Gregory politely suggested that 'more appropriate' quantitative techniques could be used to solve some of the problems discussed at the meeting. For example, he argued that linear programming should be used to determine the optimal sales/production budgets. 'Why don't we let the computer do in seconds what will take us all day? In that way we can really plan, control and evaluate various aspects of the firm.' He pointed out that the necessary calculations could be easily performed on the in-house computer.

The mini computer, with several remote terminals, is used exclusively at the present time in the financial accounting area. Recently a wide range of management accounting software had been purchased but had never been used. In an attempt to encourage wider use of the computer facilities and generate 'hands on' experience, on-line terminals had been installed in most offices in the premises.

Smith brought the meeting to a conclusion 'I think we have had a good preliminary discussion but I feel that nothing shall be resolved tonight.' He therefore proposed that a third party be asked to prepare a firm recommendation on the optimal production plan and budget for 1988. Confused over the variety of figures now available, the participants readily agreed that you were the ideal person for such a task and adjourned.

Later that evening you spend some time processing the information on the firm's computer to obtain an optimal production plan for next year (Exhibit 4). Your thoughts are interrupted by the imposing presence of Mr Smith in your office.

After exchanging greetings he explained that recently the bank manager had indicated future lending to the company might have to be curtailed. 'There will have to be some changes around here especially since we may need long-term finance,' he said. He requested a clear recommendation from you as to the best production plan for next year with related budgets. He also requested your considered advice on the various issues raised during the meeting. He was emphatic: 'Not only do I want information for the next meeting, I want ammunition as well. At future meeting I want to talk facts not fiction! And by the way, I hope you are a one armed accountant!'

Not accustomed to the term you invite explanation.

'Well,' said Smith with a faint grim, 'I don't want any accountant telling me on the one hand this and on the other hand that! Give me a straight proposal and that's the way I want our relationship to develop.'

You realise that your recommendations and observations may have important implications for certain individuals within the organisation, including yourself, and also for the firm as an entity. After refreshments appropriate to the hour, you are determined to make your report as influential and detailed as possible, with your assumptions clearly stated.

REQUIREMENT

1 Prepare a detailed budget for the forthcoming period based on the optimal solution. Do you anticipate difficulties in implementing it? Why?

2 Respond to and criticise the various arguments and proposals raised by the various participants in the discussion.

3 What are the critical assumptions and issues underlying your calculations?

Exhibit 4. Formulation and solution of linear programming problem

Objective function:	Max 5.60A + 4.00B + 6.65C
Constraint 1:	1A + 0.5B + 0.25C ≤ 120,000
2:	0.5A + 0.5B + 1.25C ≤ 100,000
3:	4A +8B + 16C ≤ 1,000,,000
4:	1A ≥ 20,000
5:	1B ≥ 15,000
6:	1C ≥ 10,000
7:	1A ≤ 110,000
8:	1B ≤ 38,000
9:	1C ≤ 20,000

Objective function value	£820,994
Alpha	96,666
Beta	36,666
Cappa	20,000

Constraint	Slack or surplus	Dual price
1	nil	4.80
2	8,334	nil
3	nil	0.20
4	76,666	nil
5	21,667	nil
6	10,000	nil
7	13,334	nil
8	1,334	nil
9	nil	2.25

Sensitivity analysis: Ranges in which the basis is unchanged:

Objective function coefficient ranges

	Current coefficient	Upper bound	Lower bound
Alpha	5.60	8.00	3.35
Beta	4.00	4.90	2.80
Cappa	6.65	inf.	4.40

Righthand side ranges

Constraint	Current rhs	Upper bound	Lower bound
1	120,000	130,000	118,000
2	100,000	inf.	91,667
3	1,000,000	1,008,000	870,000
4	20,000	96,666	inf.
5	15,000	36,666	inf.
6	10,000	20,000	inf.
7	110,000	inf.	96,667
8	38,000	inf.	36,667
9	20,000	28,666	19,467

Case 1.10 Chance Limited

In November 1987, Robert Jones, managing director of Chance Limited, was contemplating production schedules for the forthcoming year. He phoned his new accountant, Bill Davis. 'Say Bill, are you organised for tomorrow's meeting?'

Davis had been hired three months earlier as company accountant in a role which encompassed both managerial and financial functions. He was directly responsible to Jones, and until recently had been doing routine accounting work, since the company's records were considered to be in an 'awful mess' prior to his arrival. Davis was a graduate of the local business school, and subsequently qualified as an accountant. He was considered by his former employer to be talented, conscientious, but a trifle arrogant. It was this latter characteristic which generally resulted in his 'rubbing people the wrong way.' Davis was well aware of his capabilities and took advantage of every opportunity that arose to 'educate' those around him. He had recently been asked by Jones to attend the annual budget meeting and brief fellow members of the management team regarding possible production/sales strategies for the forthcoming period. Davis quickly agreed to such a request since he realised that this was his big chance to 'impress'! At long last he had the opportunity to apply some of the managerial accounting techniques that he had learned at college — CVP analysis, LP and probability theory. He thought to himself, 'I'll sock it to them!'

Chance Limited currently produces two products, namely, Alpha and Beta, each of which requires machine processing in the assembly and finishing departments of the firm. The unit selling price has already been determined for next year and it is considered that a plentiful supply of materials and labour will be available. Davis prepared the following data in relation to both products:

	Alpha	Beta
Selling price (including 10 per cent VAT)	£27.50	£36.30
Raw materials (including 10 per cent VAT)	4.40	6.60
Direct labour	8.00	12.00
Total overheads per unit	9.00	14.00
Net profit	6.10	3.70
Machine hours required per unit	Alpha	Beta
Assembly department	3	1
Finishing department	2	2

Having worked out the profit per unit and other projections, Davis realised that he had failed to segregate fixed and variable overheads. Chewing hard on his fingernails, he decided to try and bluff his way out of tomorrow's meeting. After all, he had prepared elaborate charts and schedules, and had got them photocopied for participants. Too much trouble to change things now!

One topic for the meeting was the proposal to hire, for one year, additional machinery for the assembly department at a cost of £150,000. This machinery had the identical facilities and efficiency as existing machinery, and would provide unlimited additional machine hours in that assembly department. His profit calculation to support his proposal looked good.

THE MEETING

Contributors to the meeting:

Robert Jones   Managing director
Bill Davis   Accountant
John Hunt   Production manager
Paul Byrne   Marketing manager

At the meeting, Davis talked the participants through his various calculations and projections. It soon became apparent that some of the participants had known in advance what Davis planned to discuss, and they had come prepared to 'turn the tables'.

The following exchange ensued:

John Hunt (Production manager):
Bill, I'm a little concerned about your overhead figures. According to the information that I've got here — it came from yourself — you have included both fixed and variable overheads in your profit calculations per unit. I'm not sure that such a treatment is correct for planning purposes. In addition, you show a break-even point in terms of total sales but we don't know anything about the unit sales of the individual products.'

Davis grew red in the face as he realised he was in for a rough ride from the other participants. He bit hard on his lower lip before replying.

Bill Davis (Accountant):
'Fixed overheads are a tricky one, John. I reckon that they will run at about £290,000 for the year. I assumed annual unit sales of 50,000 of each product and apportioned fixed overheads to the two products on the basis of sales revenue. OK, my break-even point may not be strictly correct but there is still a break-even point to achieve and we've got to cover our fixed costs!'

Robert Jones (Managing director):
'For the forthcoming year our production/sales planning is complicated by the existence of certain resource constraints and the pos-

41

sible marketing strategy of a rival firm who produce a similar range of products to Chance Limited. As things now stand, annual machine capacity in the assembly and finishing departments is limited to 150,000 and 200,000 hours respectively. In addition it was agreed at the previous meeting that a minimum quantity of 20,000 units of each of the two products should be produced for goodwill purposes.'

After further discussion the marketing director indicated that at current prices, there was no maximum limit on unit sales for the forthcoming year, provided the rival company did not engage in a new marketing promotion.

However the marketing strategy of the rival company is the unknown factor which must be taken into consideration in the production planning decision for next year. Jones and Byrne both felt that there was a seventy per cent probability that next year the rival company would engage in an intensive and aggressive marketing drive. In such circumstances the marketing manager suggested that the demand for Alpha and Beta would be restricted to 40,000 and 80,000 units respectively.

John Hunt (Production manager):
'There is another point which may affect your calculations. Paul Byrne and myself have been discussing the possibility of hiring that machine you suggested for £150,000 for the year. If we acquire it, then we both agree that we should introduce a new product to our range — product Gamma. We estimate that it will require only one processing hour in each of the two departments and generate a unit contribution of eight pounds. By the way, that contribution specifically excludes fixed overheads.'

Paul Byrne (Marketing manager):
I might as well get in on this. I agree with what John said about product Gamma. We know there's a definite demand for it but for short-term technical reasons we would only produce it if we acquire the additional capacity. I reckon our maximum sales would be 30,000 units of Gamma a year. However if the rival firm engages in that marketing drive as we anticipate, my maximum sales estimate for Gamma would be reduced by half. For goodwill purposes we should still produce a minimum of 20,000 units of both Alpha and Beta regardless of what happens.'

Robert Jones (Managing director):
'This meeting has certainly covered a lot of ground. Obviously, Bill, some of your figures need to be revised and a few fresh calculations need to be done. As I see it, our major decision is whether to hire the new machine for the assembly department or not. If we do, we produce three products, if we don't we stay with Alpha and Beta.

Either way our decision will be heavily influenced by the possibility of the rival firm engaging in a marketing drive next year.'

(All participants agreed with Jones' summary of the current situation)
He then continued:

'I wish we could find out what our competitors are going to do! I know it's probably illegal, but I'd be prepared to pay well for such information — provided it is one hundred per cent accurate! Anyway, Bill, will you come up with a new report for us on the alternatives which we should consider and their potential pay-offs?'

John Hunt (Production Manager):

'I have some information about Alpha and Beta which may be useful in assesing the overall risk of our alternatives. My department recently conducted a time-and-motion study on average labour costs on both products and the remarkable thing is that the probability distribution of both measurements is normally distributed. The average labour costs are the same as in Bill's schedule. However, the labour costs for both products have a standard deviation of two pounds. I think this information should be utilised to establish confidence intervals for unit contribution of both products and so forth.

Mindful of the lack of agreement among participants, it was decided to adjourn the meeting and ask Bill Davis to produce figures for an additional meeting to be held the next day.

Jones and Davis headed back to their offices and Davis in a very subdued tone asked Jones, 'Why didn't you warn me of the snake pit I was walking into?'

'Bill,' replied Jones, 'you didn't ask!'

REQUIREMENT

1 Prepare a payoff table to represent the two alternatives facing Chance Ltd and the possible marketing strategies of the rival firm. (You should assume the company wishes to maximise its profits.)

2 Determine the best strategy for the company to adopt using each of the following decision rules: (a) expected monetary value; (b) maximax; (c) maximim.

3 If Chance Ltd produces Alpha and Beta only, and the rival company does *not* engage in a marketing drive:
   (a) calculate the coefficient ranges within which the optimal production plan will remain unchanged;
   (b) what is the probability that the optimal solution (in 3a) will not change, assuming that the labour cost of product Alpha *only* is likely to fluctuate?
   (c) if the labour cost of product Beta *only* is likely to change, what

43

is the probability that the optimal solution (in 3a) will not change?

4   Assuming the directors of Chance Ltd are risk neutral, what is the maximum amount, if any, they should pay for perfect information regarding the marketing strategy of the rival company? Explain your calculations.

Note: A table for the area under the standard normal curve is presented in Appendix 2.

Case 1.11 Frank's Confectionery

In early January, the general manager of Frank's Confectionery, Frank Dwyer, called in his sales manager, Seamus Bell, to discuss marketing and production strategy for the forthcoming year.

Frank's Confectionery had been founded by Frank's father shortly after World War Two. In its early years, the firm had concentrated on producing a limited range of confectionery. Gradually the range was expanded to cater for different customer needs without reference to the underlying commercial viability. Several years ago Frank Dwyer took over the management of the company from his father and slowly began reorganisation.

When Frank joined the company it was producing about sixty individual items. Frank suspected that some items were not profitable enough to justify their continued production. Unfortunately the accounting system then operating did not provide a ready basis for deciding which items to drop, or alternatively which lines warranted special selling effort because of their attractive profit margins. Subsequently an accountant, Arthur Hughes, was employed and became an active member of Frank's management team. Within a short space of time Arthur had identified many low profit margin items and several loss markers. On Arthur's recommendation these products were immediately dropped. The cost accounting system in the confectionery was reorganised and quarterly and annual management reports were prepared showing profitability of products, which had now been grouped for convenience purposes into three main product lines. The management report for the latest financial year appears in Exhibit 1.

Exhibit 1. Management report for the year ended 31 December 1987

Product lines	A	B	C	Total
Sales	£561,000	£224,400	£336,600	£1,122,000
Material costs	224,400	90,000	135,000	449,400
Direct labour	112,200	45,000	67,000	224,200
Packaging	56,100	11,000	17,000	84,100
Electricity	5,610	2,200	3,400	11,210
Plant depreciation	30,000	12,000	18,000	60,000
General plant overheads	17,220	6,900	10,300	34,420
Distribution and advertising	45,000	18,000	27,000	90,000
Administration	70,000	28,000	42,000	140,000
Net Profit	470	11,300	16,900	28,670

On reading this management report Frank Dwyer decided to consult his sales manager to consider if it was worthwhile to retain production and sales of product line A. Frank observed that according to Hughes's figures, this product line was barely profitable. If the line was discontinued it would free capacity for the two other more profitable product lines. Before making any commitment Frank decided to get some additional information and first consulted Seamus Bell, his sales manager.

'Seamus, I want your advice about product line A,' said Frank. 'As you can see from the management accounts it has not been exactly profitable. In addition annual sales volume for the range have been fairly erratic over the past few years making it difficult to predict things for next year. I don't really know what we should do about it.'

In advance of the meeting Seamus Bell had gathered some important information. 'Well first of all I don't agree that sales have been erratic,' responded Bell. 'In fact sales average just under 55,000 units for the past ten years. Look.' Seamus produced a table of previous sales levels (Exhibit 2). He added, 'There will always be some uncertainty about the number of units of each product which we'll sell in any year, but we can use this uncertainty to our advantage.' He paused for effect, then continued, 'Our sales pattern is referred to in statistical terms as a normal distribution. We only came across this point the other day in my MBA class. Using this normal distribution I could calculate the probability of breaking even on this product line next year. Alternatively if you want to reduce your risk exposure I can work out the probability of incurring a loss of, say, £5,000. There are lots of probabilities I could work out — provided of course I had good cost data to go on!'

Exhibit 2. Product line A — annual sales data

Year	Sales (units)
1978	50,800
1979	49,100
1980	57,600
1981	51,800
1982	54,600
1983	61,500
1984	54,600
1985	50,600
1986	59,300
1987	56,100
Average	54,600

Seamus Bell then began complaining about the product line costings produced by the accounting department under the responsibility of Arthur Hughes. 'Its no wonder that this line is considered to be unprofitable; it has been charged for everything from depreciation of equipment to a share of postage costs. The only real expense in producing these

46

items are materials and labour, but Hughes doesn't seem to realise that fact. If we include these two costs only in our analysis then the product range becomes very profitable and should be retained.'

Frank Dwyer, being a reasonable and intelligent person, was prepared to carefully consider arguments both in favour of and against the continuance of product line A. However, before trying to make up his own mind about Bell's observations on costs, Frank asked Arthur Hughes to explain the basis of the various cost apportionments and allocations which appeared in the management accounting report. The following day, just in time for coffee, Arthur appeared in Frank's office to discuss the rationale behind his costings.

Arthur began his explanation by stating that all costs incurred by the company had to be apportioned among the various product lines. Materials, labour and packaging costs were fairly straightforward since they were traceable to individual product lines and as a result they tended to increase or decrease as product or sales volume moved up or down. Electricity costs were also primarily variable in nature and fluctuated on a fairly consistent basis with direct labour cost. General plant overheads excluding depreciation were a mixture of product and period costs. So for planning control purposes a flexible budget formula is operated. The variable element in general plant overhead works out at ten per cent of labour cost. The fixed element is apportioned to each product line on the basis of sales revenue.

In relation to the other costs Arthur stated that nobody could calculate the precise amount attributable to each product line. It was inevitable that any such allocation was arbitrary but at least he tried to allocate costs on a consistent basis and one that was reasonable and fair. 'After all,' he explained, 'if there was no consistency, our management accounting reports would not be comparable between accounting periods and therefore useless for analysis and discussion purposes. For example, plant depreciation which is basically a fixed cost is apportioned on the basis of sales revenue which is an eminently fair basis. Likewise distribution, advertising and administration expenses being in the nature of committed, common costs, are apportioned on the basis of revenue. These costs wouldn't exist if we weren't in business and they are just as much a part of the total cost of the goods produced as materials and labour. They appear on our profit and loss account and unless our prices take account of them, we would be operating at a loss.'

Arthur, as always, was convincing, thought Frank. He was in command of his subject and had a way with words whereby one automatically accepted what he said. However, Frank was a little uneasy about the underlying cost apportionment process and how it had the potential to distort the profitability performance of the different product lines. He was concerned about the methods of apportionment and why they were chosen. He realised that different apportionment methods were likely to generate different figures. Yet, Frank acknowledged Hughes' argument that all costs have to be taken into consideration in making product decisions. Frank admitted to himself that he was more confused than enlightened.

In spite of his conversation with Hughes, Frank felt that he was still no wiser as to whether product line A should be continued or discontinued in the forthcoming year. The selling price, he agreed with Bell could not be raised without adversely affecting sales volume. As a result the selling price would remain unchanged. Moreover there was no scope for the reduction in costs either through increased efficiency or changes in raw material composition. If at all possible Frank would like to see the line continued especially since it produced the highest sales revenue. Hughes had made no clear recommendation on whether the line should be continued or discontinued. Frank could not help but think that Arthur had deliberately fudged the issue.

REQUIREMENT

1 Prepare a schedule for management showing the relative profitability of the individual product lines. Explain your workings.

2 What justification does Seamus Bell have in suggesting that the annual sales level of product line A is normally distributed?

3 If product line A is continued, what is the probability of it breaking even? Of generating a contribution of £162,000 or more?

4 What is the expected impact on profits if product line A is discontinued. What other factors should be considered in addition to your calculations in making a final decision?

Note: The standard deviation is a most important measure of dispersion and is denoted by σ. The standard deviation is found by:
- (a) squaring the deviations of individual values from the arithmetic mean where $\bar{x}$ represents the mean;
- (b) adding the squared deviations together;
- (c) dividing this sum by the number of items in the distribution;
- (d) taking the square root of the value in (c).

The basic formula is as follows:

$$\sqrt{\frac{E\,(x-\bar{x})^2}{N}}$$

Case 1.12 Braincell Limited

Early in 1987, both the chief executive and marketing manager of Braincell Limited met to discuss pricing recommendations for its two principle products for the forthcoming year. Braincell manufactures and distributes two household cleaning and polishing compounds, regular and heavy duty, under the Easi-clean label. The chief executive, Gus Finucane was appointed to the company several years ago and was the dominant personality in the company. All important decisions concerning the company were personally approved by him before being implemented.

In previous years, after they both had agreed on selling prices they would submit their recommendations to the board of directors for approval. Normally their fellow directors would accept their recommendations without argument or question. Indeed the function of board meeting was largely an exercise in diplomacy rather than decision-making. The company subsequently announced the prices for the forthcoming year in circulars to its regular and potential customers. In accordance with company and industry practice, announced prices were adhered to for the year unless radical changes in the market occurred — a rare event. Finucane realised that the pricing recommendations for next year would have to be made before the board meeting at the end of the month.

The heavy and regular duty compounds were the only products currently being produced by Braincell. Last year the company raised the price of both products by ten per cent in order to increase overall company profitability. Although the company had a fairly healthy balance sheet, additional funds would soon be required to finance the proposed modernisation and expansion scheme of the company. The selling price increase, implemented at the start of last year, had been one of the changes advocated by Finucane in an attempt to improve the company's cash flow situation.

However, as a result of these price increases the company had lost a fairly significant proportion of its dominant market position in both products. The marketing manager, Jim Ward, strongly expressed the opinion that a further decline in market share could take place unless prices for next year were reduced and thus made competitive. However Finucane was not convinced that the demand for both the company's products were necessarily price sensitive. Most of Braincell's competitors were relatively small producers. As a result they usually waited for Braincell to announce its prices before finalising their own pricing arrangements. Last year however they held their prices stable despite Braincell's price increases and Braincell's overall market share declined accordingly.

Current selling prices and annual sales volume of Braincell's products are as follows:

Product	Sales price (per case)	Sales (in cases)
Regular compound	£11.40	140,000
Heavy duty compound	£18.70	70,000

Percentage mark up on cost is the basis of Braincell's current policy in relation to the pricing of both products. The fundamental consideration in pricing policy is the total cost of each product, the ascertainment of which is the responsibility of the accounting department headed by Mike Harvey. The costs attributable to each product ascertained by Harvey are obtained by the use of absorption or full costing. To these cost figures are added a fixed percentage; fifty per cent in the case of the regular compound and twenty-five per cent in relation to heavy duty. There didn't seem to be any strong rationale behind the choice of the rate selected. Rather the rates chosen were 'in use for several years'. Nobody seemed to know when these mark-ups were originally established or for what reason. The computed selling prices were then adjusted by a relatively small amount to take into consideration factors such as psychological prices, since a selling price of £11.40 was more attractive to the customer to the customer than, say, £11.43.

Gus Finucane had made attempts to consider possible alternatives to the cost-based attitude to pricing. However his efforts were of no avail since Harvey typically replied, 'We have no other starting point for price determination!' If pressed further he would inevitably respond, 'Our selling prices must cover costs if we want to make profits.'

Finucane had attended recently a seminar in the local business school on managerial accounting techniques for decision-making purposes with special emphasis on pricing policy. One of the points made frequently at the seminar was the need to initially analyse and segregate expenses by their fixed and variable elements for decision-making purposes. The seminar had also stressed the concept of 'profit maximisation' which was achieved through pricing policy when 'marginal revenue' equated with 'marginal cost.' Finucane grasped the importance of these concepts and now realised the basic error contained in full cost pricing adopted by his company. The basic problem lay in the way that Harvey calculated total cost for each product. To determine one unit cost, the accounting department first calculated the number of units to be produced and sold and, based on these estimates, a portion of fixed cost was allocated to each product. The paradox, Finucane thought, was that to determine the full cost-plus selling price of an item one must first fix the number to be sold — yet Finucane understood that the selling price of a product determined the number of units sold rather than *vice versa!*

Finucane was particularly interested in the application of the profit maximisation concept to pricing decisions in his company. Upon his return to the office, Finucane discussed the seminar's proceedings with his marketing manager, Jim Ward. They decided to consider seriously alternative approaches to pricing for the company's two products. Ward argued, and Finucane agreed, that any pricing computation should start off with consideration being given to anticipated sales demand at alternative price levels. Ward indicated that according to his research each successive fifty pence price increase per case for regular compounds would reduce annual sales by 5,000 units and each successive price decrease of fifty pence per case would give a similar increase. For the heavy duty compound each successive price change of thirty pence would give a 2,500 change in cases sold in both directions. Ward explained that although his research was carried out on the basis of fifty pence and thirty pence changes it was possible to charge intermediary prices within these ranges for both products with proportionate changes in demand. Thus any selling price was possible he added, even if it meant changing the selling price of each product by a few pence. After Ward explained the implications of the research, Finucane finally accepted that the sales demand for both products was price sensitive and that the situation could and should be exploited if at all possible. Ward was confident that competitors would not reduce their selling prices even if Braincell did so. His argument was based on the premise that, being relatively smaller companies, they all had higher operating costs than Braincell and selling price reductions on their part would eliminate their profitability. Likewise they would retain their current selling prices even if Braincell increased theirs.

As a result of a request from Finucane the accounting department under the directions of Harvey, had produced estimates of total costs for both products at various levels of production (Exhibit 1 and 2). They were largely based on past experience but were considered representative of what could be anticipated next year. It was anticipated that there would be no difficulty in hiring additional labour of equal ability

Exhibit 1. Estimated cost per case — regular compound

Number of cases	80,000	100,000	120,000	140,000	160,000	180,000
Raw material	£1.00	£1.00	£1.00	£1.00	£1.00	£1.00
Direct labour	2.00	2.00	2.00	2.00	2.00	2.00
Production overhead	1.67	1.44	1.28	1.20	1.12	1.07
Factory cost	4.67	4.44	4.28	4.20	4.12	4.07
Administration etc	5.00	4.20	3.71	3.40	3.13	2.95
Total cost	9.67	8.64	7.99	7.60	7.25	7.02

in producing either product if required. This was because the labour input to each product was largely unskilled and there was a plentiful supply in the locality. Moreover existing staff could be let go if necessary.

Exhibit 2. Estimated cost per case — heavy duty compound

Number of cases	50,000	60,000	70,000	80,000	90,000
Raw material	£1.00	£1.00	£1.00	£1.00	£1.00
Direct labour	4.00	4.00	4.00	4.00	4.00
Production overhead	3.30	2.90	2.56	2.26	2.15
Factory cost	8.30	7.90	7.56	7.26	7.15
Administration etc	10.00	8.50	7.41	6.53	6.20
Total cost	18.30	16.40	14.97	13.79	13.35

The production manager, Kevin Dooley, was called to Finucane's office to discuss the production and pricing issues. He explained that both products were produced on a separate production line. This enabled total production overheads to be correctly allocated to the two products. The total production overhead attributable to each product is divided by output to provide average production cost per unit. While normal manufacturing capacity is generally about 140,000 cases of regular compound and 70,000 cases of heavy duty compound, the plant is capable of producing 180,000 cases of regular compound and 90,000 cases of heavy duty compound annually. There was no difficulty, he added in producing any quantity below these limits. Any level of output at or below maximum levels was feasible he confirmed.

When a possible change in pricing policy was suggested to him, Dooley was sceptical. The present system, he stated, had worked well in the past and the profits of the company were satisfactory. It appeared logical to him that selling prices should be set to cover costs and this policy had resulted in relatively stable prices in the past. A new pricing policy could produce more volatile selling prices and if that was the case it would be difficult to predict how competitors would react. He concluded; 'For my money, stick to what you know!'

REQUIREMENT

1 What factors should normally be considered in arriving at a pricing decision?

2 Based on data in Exhibits 1 and 2, compute selling prices on a mark-up basis and compare with sales prices which Jim Ward thinks are necessary to sell the required quantities. Comment on your findings.

3   Based on the data, advise on the prices for each product to be charged in order to maximise profits. What is the maximum profit level?

4   What selling prices of each product would maximise revenues? Calculate profits at these levels. To what extent are profit maximisation and sales maximisation objectives compatible in this instance?

Case 1.13 Industrial Chemicals

Ray Ward the managing director of Industrial Chemicals, was a little puzzled by the memorandum which he had just read (Exhibit 1). Prepared jointly by the marketing and production managers, it contained a capital expenditure proposal which was capable of increasing company profitability — provided of course the figures were correct. Ward was a trained chemical engineer and he had complemented this with an MBA degree. In a career spanning twenty years in the chemical industry, he had held a variety of positions in different firms. It was such experience which had landed him the post of managing director with Industrial Chemicals a few years ago.

Industrial Chemicals was an Irish based subsidiary of an American multinational corporation. It was founded in the 1960s to manufacture a variety of chemicals for industrial use. As a result of rationalisation during the 1970s the company became a speciality chemical company and which now produced a single brand of chemical used in the resource extraction industry. This product is sold both on the domestic and foreign markets.

The chemical production operation consists of two distinct processes. Initially a four-gallon container is filled with two gallons of Alpha and two gallons of Omega. The liquids are gradually mixed at a constant but low temperature. Alpha and Omega are the only direct raw materials in the production process at this mixing stage and cost £2 and £4 per gallon respectively. Each four-gallon input is attributed with £1 for variable labour and mixing department overhead.

The mixture is then transferred to another department for separation by a conventional boiling process known as fractional distillation. Attributable separation costs are estimated at fifty pence per gallon of input. Because of the high temperature involved, ten per cent of the liquid input is lost through evaporation and is not retrievable. The separation process results in two different liquids. One is a light substance which represents the commercial chemical which is sold to consumers. This commercial chemical typically represents eighty per cent of the output of the separation process. The other liquid is a much heavier variety and represents a residue in the form of sediments and impurities. This liquid residue is smelly and chemically unstable and was considered by senior managers in Industrial Chemicals to be more a nuisance than anything else. However, there was a market for this residue and Ward was pleased to be able to sell it as a by-product at £2 per gallon to another chemical manufacturer.

Aiden Daly, marketing manager of the company had been pushing strongly in recent weeks for Ward's approval for this proposal to install a solvent-conversion unit (SCU) in the plant. The equipment, together

Exhibit 1.

MEMORANDUM

To: Ray Ward, managing director

From: Aiden Daly (marketing) and Brian Burns (production)

Re: Further processing of liquid residue to convert into marketable 'RFP' (residue further processed).

 The following is a summary of our capital expenditure proposal. Our detailed workings and assumptions can be discussed with you later.

1.	Investment cost	£200,000 (delivered and installed) for solvent conversion unit
2.	Economic life	4 years
3.	Production process	To produce 'RFP', one-half gallon of additional chemicals will be added at the start of processing in the solvent-conversion unit to each gallon of residue received from the cooling process. After processing thirty per cent of the total mixture represents effluent and has no commercial value. The remainder will be containerised and sold
4.	Sales price	Our own market research confirms an adequate and growing market for 'RFP' which will be sold at £4 per gallon

5. Additional production/conversion costs

Additional chemicals required	£2 per gallon added at the start of processing
Processing costs of solvent	40p per gallon of liquid put into conversion process
Labour cost	£40,000 per annum
Sales commission	10 per cent of sales price
Advertising	£200,000 (immediate outlay)
Sales representatives	£28,000 per annum. (1 representative only)

6.	Scrap value of equipment	£20,000 (after four years)

with modifications to the building and allowing for delivery and installation, was expected to be £200,000. The function of such a unit would be to purify the residual liquid and further process it in-house to produce a marketable product which was initially referred to as RFP. There appeared to be no alternative to purchasing the equipment; none of the existing equipment could be adopted to perform the necessary operations, neither could the equipment be rented.

Ward recalled that the proposal to install a solvent conversion unit had been seriously considered by him and his fellow directors of Industrial Chemicals some time ago but a decision had been postponed because the production process was judged to need additional development and refinement. Subsequently the research and development department of Industrial Chemicals had confirmed the feasability of this production operation. Indeed they had spent close to £18,000 researching and developing the production process. The conversion process had been thoroughly tested and patented. Now the decision to go ahead or abandon the idea could be based on financial criteria.

Ward was intrigued with Daly's proposal. It represented an excellent opportunity to open up a potentially significant new market segment. The company had plans to put 1,000,000 gallons of liquid into the normal mixing operations during each of the next four years. He knew from experience that this would automatically result in liquid residue of significant amounts. Thus the supply of raw material for the conversion unit was therefore, reasonably well assured.

To support his proposal Daly had conducted basic market research since he was not prepared to let his own enthusiasm sway his judgement. He had pressed several potential customers to provide written evidence of their reaction to the new product, designated 'RFP'. To his surprise, he had been able to obtain a written committment from two potential customers to purchase specific quantities which meant, in effect, fifty per cent of the production of 'RFP' in the next four years was presold. Based on this response Daly felt it was feasible that the entire projected output or 'RFP' would be sold. Daly also informed Ward that a few similar chemical companies in the UK had already gone ahead with the solvent-conversion unit, so it must be a good investment. Ward sensed that now might be a good time to invest. The industry to which 'RFP' would be sold was booming. In addition the company had some spare funds available for an investment project such as this, although not quiet of the magnitude required.

Experience had taught Ward that decisions of such magnitude could only be taken after extensive analysis of the underlying financial data. The essential factor was to ensure that the proposal was financially viable. If it was such a good idea the numbers would show it and Ward would then submit the idea to his board of directors. At a minimum each capital expenditure proposal was required to contain the following:

1. A description of the proposal including a statement why the investment was necessary.
2. Estimated cost for the project.
3. Projection of additional revenues resulting from the investment, or alternatively cost savings.
4. Estimated life of the project and anticipated scrap values.
5. A calculation of the following capital expenditure analysis values:
   (a) payback period;
   (b) projected net present value using a hurdle rate of 16 per cent after tax;
   (c) project's present value (PV) index;
   (d) project's internal rate of return.

To firm up on some additional details of the proposal Ward had passed a copy of the memo to Jim Kavanagh, the financial controller, for his initial comments. Kavanagh responded quickly and pointed out that no recognition had been made of tax payments or the possibility of government grants being received. Although the company's corporation tax rate was ten per cent, nevertheless the taxation implications of the proposal had to be considered. For example, he explained that the total investment in new fixed assets would qualify for immediate write off for tax purposes. Thus tax payments on any profits generated in the early years could be effectively postponed for some time. In addition, investment in new manufacturing assets, such as the conversion unit, would qualify for a forty per cent government grant. This grant would be normally received one year after approval. These two factors would increase the overall attractiveness of the proposal.

However Kavanagh did indicate that if the proposal was implemented, the new product would automatically be allocated a 'fair share' of general fixed production overhead. Currently, the overheads of £950,000 were apportioned between the mixing and separating departments on the basis of gallons of input to each department. If 'RFP' is to be manufactured, a reallocation of cost would be made and the solvent-conversion unit charged an amount per gallon of input to reflect its fair share. Ward wondered whether this allocation of general production overhead would make the proposal less attractive. Since his background included very little training in the area of managerial accounting he was unsure of the correct answer.

Another issue concerning the proposal bothered Ward. The economic life of the project was estimated at four years because at the end of that period the entire investment in equipment for the conversion process would have to be replaced. Thus the project would probably require another large investment in four years' time. A remarkably short life span, thought Ward. The replacement in four years would come at a critical period for the company since it already had strategic plans to commit large sums to other capital projects at that time, involving a gradual diversification into business segments outside the current production orientation.

Ward's mind kept wandering in anticipation of the forthcoming meeting of the board of directors in two weeks' time. It was at this meeting that he could make a presentation of the proposal since the US parent company had always insisted on a formal process for submitting capital expenditure requests in excess of £100,000. He knew that a recommendation from him would be taken quite seriously by his fellow directors. He was most anxious to be able to present a convincing and substantiated case in financial terms for whatever recommendation he finally made.

REQUIREMENT

1   How attractive, in financial terms, is the proposed investment? Explain your figures.

2   What are the major issues to be considered in either accepting or rejecting the proposal?

3   What valuation would you place on each unsold gallon of 'RFP' at the end of the first year for stock valuation purposes? How does this figure differ from that used in your analysis? Explain.

Case 1.14 Rafter and Company

In early January 1988 Rafter and Company a small family-owned business, had grown to a point where it was operating at full capacity. The company was producing and selling a single household product which was considered a brand leader in its field.

Consequently, David Rafter, owner and manager of the company, was contemplating renting long term new cutting equipment for his production operation. The existing equipment was several years old and in poor condition. It required extensive maintenance and repairs to keep it operational. The annual repair and maintenance bill for machinery was considered by Rafter to be excessive. Unfortunately the warranty period had expired. Replacing the cutting machine now with a more up to date model made good economic sense, he argued to himself without having the necessary detailed facts to substantiate his opinion. Because this new cutting equipment would increase production capacity it would enable the introduction of a new product catering for the industrial and commercial market. Rafter had made enquiries about the new cutting equipment and had provisionally agreed its rental for a four-year period with annual payments of £30,000. However Rafter had one week to make a final decision about the rental contract. He realised that such an acquisition would have a significant impact on the cash flow position of the company over the next four years.

Until now expenditure decisions for new equipment had been made without any proper financial analysis. This was mainly due to the fact that the sums involved were fairly small in relation to the resources of the company. Once David Rafter decided, or was convinced by his colleagues, that a new piece of equipment was needed, it was purchased. No formal economic justification had ever been required to support capital expenditure proposals. However, Rafter realised that the amount of money to be invested in this proposal, required that it be scrutinised very carefully. Once committed to the project there was no turning back.

Rafter and Company was a profitable business by the standards of many small, Irish private companies. It provided a generous living for Rafter and his family. The company had long been regarded as a well-managed company. It had succeeded in keeping its product to the forefront of the market and it had maintained its position in a highly competitive industry.

The product was produced from raw materials purchased from a supplier based in the United Kingdom. These raw materials were initially machine-cut in the cutting department and then sent to the finishing department for final machine processing. Due to the nature of the raw material there was no spoilage or wastage. Moreover defective units produced were simply reprocessed. The company produced to order so that opening and closing stock levels were virtually negligible. However extended trade credit was granted to customers which often resulted in the company having periodic cash flow problems.

Relevant financial and operating data for the existing household product, together with the latest balance sheet is presented in Exhibits 1 to 3.

Exhibit 1. Income statement for year ended 31 December 1987

Sales (10,000 units)		£200,000
Cost of sales		
Direct materials	£100,000	
Direct labour	30,000	
Total production overhead: cutting	18,000	
Total production overhead: finishing	21,000	169,000
Gross profit		31,000
Selling and distribution	16,000	
Administration	7,000	
Financial	3,000	26,000
Net profit		5,000

Exhibit 2. Balance sheet at 31 December 1987

Fixed assets (net)	£48,000	Ordinary share capital	£10,000
		Revenue reserves	60,000
Net current assets	42,000	8% debentures	20,000
	90,000		90,000

Exhibit 3. Operating data

Machine processing time per unit:	
cutting department	30 minutes
finishing department	30 minutes
Maximum operating machine time:	
cutting department	5,000 hours per annum
assembly department	8,000 hours per annum

The proposal which David Rafter was now considering concerned the replacement of all existing machinery in the cutting department which was already operating at maximum capacity. He estimated that existing machinery had a remaining productive life of four years. Extensive maintenance expenditure over each of the next four years would ensure that the annual operating capacity of the cutting department remained at 5,000 machine hours per annum. The machinery to be replaced stands in the books at £24,000 having cost £36,000 when acquired a few years ago. At present it has a scrap value of £6,000 while its value in four years time will be virtually negligible. The new equipment would be rented over four years with annual payments of £30,000.

The acquisition of the new cutting equipment would double existing capacity in that department only and for each of the next four years. It will also affect current annual maintenance costs by reducing them by £4,000 per annum. However the proposed investment in cutting machinery would not otherwise affect the level of fixed costs.

The additional capacity in the cutting department would enable the expansion of the company's product line to include a cheaper but easier to produce industrial product. Rafter has been contemplating the production of such a product for some time but lack of capacity has prevented it. The introduction of a new product would be diversification: an appropriate strategy in the present climate. Rafter realises that to have 'all his eggs in one basket' is a potential recipe for disaster.

With the new cutting equipment Rafter would be able to produce two products, one for household and one for industrial/commercial use. The industrial product would be produced from the same type of raw materials but its production was entirely conditional on the acquisition

Exhibit 4. Revised classification of overheads, year ended 31 December 1987

Cost item	Variable*	Fixed	Total
Cutting department – overhead			
Depreciation (5,000 machine hours)	£6,000	nil	£6,000
Maintenance and repairs	1,000	£4,000	5,000
Rates and insurance	nil	1,000	1,000
Indirect labour	nil	3,000	3,000
Power	2,500	500	3,000
	9,500	8,500	18,000
Finishing department – overhead			
Depreciation (5,000 machine hours)	5,000	nil	5,000
Maintenance and repairs	500	1,500	2,000
Rates and insurance	nil	1,000	1,000
Indirect labour	nil	5,000	5,000
Power	5,000	3,000	8,000
	10,500	10,500	21,000
Selling and distribution	10,000	6,000	16,000
Administration	nil	7,000	7,000
Financial	nil	3,000	3,000

*Variable in relation to machine hours.

of the new equipment. Basic data for the industrial product is as follows:

Sales price per unit	£15
Direct materials	6
Direct labour	3

However, Rafter is not sure how the overheads would work out for his new product. The new industrial product would share the same production facilities as the household product. It would also require thirty minutes of machine time in the cutting department and only 20 minutes in the finishing department since a highly finished product was not necessary.

In order to sort out the data to perform a proper financial analysis, David rearranged the cost data from his recent income statement so that it portrayed both the fixed and variable components of the overall level of costs (Exhibit 4). Direct labour and direct materials were excluded since Rafter believed these to be one hundred per cent variable.

After a recent discussion with his production manager, David Rafter was not so sure about the proposal. The production manager, Jack Ryan, agrued that there was nothing to be gained from the proposed acquisition and that it would be pointless to dispose of fixed assets at a loss before their useful life expires. To support his argument he produced the following schedule:

loss on existing equipment (£24,000 – £6,000)	£(18,000)
less: saving on maintenance (£4,000 x 4 years)	16,000
loss on investment	(2,000)

Rafter wasn't quiet sure how to respond to this argument. But he admitted that it looked logical and convincing when written down on paper. However before a final decision was made all the data needed to be properly analysed.

REQUIREMENT

1   Criticise the schedule produced by the production manager.

2   If the proposed acquisition of new cutting equipment takes place what is the optimal production plan? Explain your figures.

3   What is the payback period for this proposal?

4   Based on net present value, would you recommend the investment to take place? Why? Explain your choice of the cost of capital.

Note: Ignore taxation.

Part 2

Budgetary control,
standard costing and evaluation
of performance through variances

Case 2.1 Medical Suppliers Limited

Frank Roche, managing director of Medical Suppliers Limited was depressed and annoyed as he reviewed his firm's draft financial statements for the accounting year ended 31 December 1987. His operating profit for the year, although reasonably satisfactory, was well below that which he had anticipated. Moreover towards the end of the year the firm had begun to experience cash flow problems which resulted in his bank manager threatening to dishonour the company's cheques due to lack of funds, just before Christmas. Fortunately for Roche, the bank manager mellowed with the Christmas spirit and postponed taking any action until the new year. Roche was annoyed though, not by the bad news itself, but by the suddeness and lack of advance notice. The problem, Roche decided, was the lack of an adequate financial planning and control system within the company. If one existed it would be possible to compare actual results with budgets on a regular and frequent basis and take corrective action where necessary.

Medical Suppliers Limited was founded by Frank Roche, a veterinary surgeon, several years ago. As a result of research undertaken by him, supported and funded through the local university, the company was established to manufacture animal fertility diagnostic kits. The kits consisted of a special oesterone sulphate test for diagnosing late pregnancy in cattle. Such testing facilities are particularly important to the Irish beef industry. Generally, animals thought to be infertile would be sent for slaughter. These diagnostic testing kits (Kit A) could confirm pregnancy and thus prevent the loss of the animal and its calf. The product was an instant success and sales growth has been impressive.

Encouraged by the success of its only product, the researchers at Medical Suppliers Limited developed a second diagnostic kit (Kit B) to test the number of piglets being carried by a pregnant sow. It is very important to be able to estimate the potential litter size in pig farming since small litters are generally uneconomic. Encouraged by positive market research findings the diagnostic fertility kit for pigs was launched two years ago. Since then sales targets have been exceeded and the demand for the product continues to grow. However, this growth in sales and working capital requirements has placed inevitable liquidity strains on the company.

By the start of the new year Roche was determined to ensure that his company would not run short of cash again during the forthcoming year. The only way to prevent undesired happenings was to adopt a budgetary control system within the firm, detailing revenues and operating expenses. Roche planned to have meetings with heads of departments at which the results for the previous quarter would be discussed and reviewed. In that way unfavourable trends could be corrected.

65

The first step was to establish quarterly budgets for the year and to this end Roche called a meeting for the first day back to work after Christmas. He began by outlining the unsatisfactory nature of the current accounting and information system and then explained what he proposed to do for the forthcoming year. Roche explained that he wanted to introduce a budgetary control system, not to penalise managers, but to help them and him run the business more efficiently. He pointed out that at present nobody knew where the company was going in financial terms. Indeed, he added that it required a few pre-Christmas phone calls from the bank manager to bring home the inadequacy (and seriousness) of the company's situation. The company was generating profits but not sufficient cash. Without sufficient cash flow the company's research and development activities would have to be curtailed. To reinforce his argument Roche presented all participants with the firm's latest balance sheet (Exhibit 1).

The first item in the budgetary process to be agreed was sales quotas for the year. The marketing manager argued that it was reasonable to assume a twenty per cent increase in sales volume for both products compared with the corresponding quarter in the previous year. This growth estimate was typical of what had happened in previous years.

Following a brief discussion the sales quotas per quarter for 1988 were agreed as follows:

	Kit A (units)	Kit B (units)
Quarter 1 (Jan–Mar)	21,600	24,000
Quarter 2 (Apr–Jun)	40,000	32,000
Quarter 3 (Jul–Sept)	65,000	30,000
Quarter 4 (Oct–Dec)	14,400	30,000
	141,000	116,000

It was accepted that the sales price would remain the same as last year which was £5 for Kit A and £3 for Kit B. Both selling prices were exclusive of VAT at ten per cent. The cash flow implications of the above figures were queried, especially since customers, on average, take two months' credit. After some discussion it was decided that existing credit terms would continue since any curtailment could adversely affect sales growth. In any event, it was difficult enough to get cash out of customers in the present climate.

Discussion then centered on production and raw material requirements. In order to avoid the risk of stock-outs it was decided to carry stocks of both finished kits at a level equivalent to the following quarter's forecasted sales. In turn it was decided to maintain stocks of raw materials equivalent to the following quarter's production requirements. It was acknowledged that the planned investment in working capital would place additional liquidity strains on the company. It was

Exhibit 1. Draft balance sheet at 31 December 1987

Fixed assests at cost		£100,000
Less: aggregate depreciation		(30,000)
		70,000
Current assets:		
Stocks — raw materials (Kit A)	£40,000	
raw materials (Kit B)	20,000	
finished goods (Kit A)	45,000	
finished goods (Kit B)	30,000	
Debtors	99,000	234,000
		304,000
Financed by:		
Share capital		80,000
Revenue reserves		54,000
		134,000
Current liabilities:		
Creditors	24,000	
Bank overdraft	140,000	
VAT payable (Nov–Dec)	6,000	170,000
		304,000

Accounting policies:
1 Stocks:
  (i) raw materials are valued at cost of purchase
  (ii) finished goods are valued at variable cost of production.
2 Depreciation:
  depreciation is provided on fixed assets at the rate of twenty per cent per annum on cost. A full year's depreciation is provided in year of acquisition but none in year of sale.

an expensive strategy as current overdraft rates were ten per cent per annum. Nevertheless the company, being in a growth phase could not afford the risk of being unable to satisfy unanticipated demand. The firm's chief supplier was approached and asked to extend its credit terms from 45 days to 90 days. Eventually new credit terms were agreed provided the company paid an extra ten per cent for goods purchased. The agreement with the chief supplier would take effect from the 1 January.

The accountant then produced details of the main expense headings involved in administration and production (Exhibit 2). He explained that the firm operated a marginal costing system. When queried about this practice he replied that fixed costs, including depreciation, were written off immediately to the profit and loss account rather than being partly apportioned to closing stock. From the expression on the faces of participants it was obvious than nobody really understood what he was talking about. However, nobody was inclined to pursue the matter.

Exhibit 2.

General expenses (total)			
Administration expenses	£3,000 per month		
Selling expenses	One per cent of sales price, excluding VAT		
Research and development expenditure	£5,000 per month		

Operating expenses		Kit A	Kit B
Raw materials (including ten per cent VAT) per kit		88p	66p
Labour hours		20 mins	10 mins
Labour rate per hour		£6	£6
Variable overhead per kit		20p	40p

The plant manager mentioned that the only operating constraint to be faced during the forthcoming year was the shortage of production labour. The maximum available labour for production was 4,000 hours per quarter. Any additional hours above this had to be paid at a premium of twenty-five per cent according to union agreements. As an alternative it was neither possible or practical to take on additional employees to cope with excess production requirements.

The final issue to be discussed was the proposed acquisition of new research equipment. The company was committed to an extensive research programme which required expensive equipment. The equipment was due to be purchased in early July. The participants were horrified to learn that the cost of £20,000 didn't even include VAT at the rate of twenty-five per cent.

Roche rounded off the meeting by saying, 'Okay, let's see what it all comes to. I'll put together a tentative budget proposal and circulate it to you all for your comments.'

REQUIREMENT

1   Prepare a quarterly cash budget and income statement for the year ended 31 December 1988, together with a balance sheet as at that date.

2   What steps could be taken to improve the cash flow position of the firm?

3   Assuming the employees were unable (or unwilling) to work overtime, what production schedule would you recommend? Why?

4   Briefly explain the impact on your reported profits if the firm used an absorption costing system.

Case 2.2 Eastern Oil Company

Patrick Murphy, managing director of the Eastern Oil Company, had just instructed his secretary to hold all calls and cancel his remaining appointments for the afternoon. He admitted privately that he had shouted his instructions — most unusual behaviour for him. The cause of this uncharacteristic outburst was that he had just spoken to the company's bank manager who had flatly refused Murphy's polite request for additional credit facilities to carry the firm over its current 'cash flow difficulties'. Indeed the bank manager had refused to even discuss additional bank loans until some form of reasonable financial projections were prepared by Eastern Oil for next year.

Murphy was a supreme pragmatist. 'If that's what the manager wants, that's what he'll get,' he said resolutely to himself.

The Eastern Oil Company had grown dramatically since its incorporation in 1971 and was now a large, independent distributor of oil for domestic and commercial central heating systems. The dynamic growth in sales volume over the past years was attributable to a number of factors. Firstly, Murphy was a charismatic character and well known in the locality, especially for his sporting exploits. Secondly, Eastern Oil was competitive in price terms. Currently their selling price of 110p per gallon (inclusive of ten per cent VAT) was at least two or three pence cheaper than potential rivals. Finally, the terms of trade offered by Eastern Oil were attractive to customers. Eastern Oil guaranteed delivery of oil within twenty-four hours of order. This meant keeping a relatively large fleet of trucks and drivers but it was considered necessary if a prompt delivery service was to be maintained. In addition, customers were never pressed for cash on delivery but were simply requested to 'send a cheque in as soon as possible.'

In an attempt to generate some financial projections for next year, Murphy requested both the company accountant and sales manager to stay late that evening for a brief meeting. The purpose of holding the meeting after hours was that there would be no interruptions so that the participants could devote their full attention to the budgeting exercise. The two key managers were Tony Cox who was in charge of sales and Pat Brady who was in charge of the accounting function.

It was most unusual for key managers to be summoned simultaneously to Murphy's office for a meeting. Sensing their apprehension on arrival, Murphy began by outlining his discussion earlier that day with the company's bank manager. He stressed that the polite refusal of additional credit facilities should not be viewed in a negative way but rather as an incentive to institute some form of budgetary control procedures in the company. 'After all,' said Murphy, 'we should know where we're going and be able to monitor our progress towards that end.' Forward planning had not been previously adopted by Eastern Oil but the past eighteen months had seen a variety of problems which might well have been avoided had it been in operation. The severity of the current liquidity crisis, for example, had convinced Murphy of the desirability of a budgetary control system.

The liquidity problem of the company was very apparent from the latest balance sheet (Exhibit 1).

Exhibit 1. Balance Sheet at 30 June 1987

EASTERN OIL LIMITED

Fixed assets	Cost	Agg. Depr.	
Buildings	£100,000	£30,000	£70,000
Vehicles	60,000	21,000	39,000
Equipment	12,000	7,500	4,500
	172,000	58,500	113,500
Current assets			
Stock at cost		32,000	
Accounts receivable		26,400	
		58,400	
Less: Current liabilities			
Bank overdraft	61,000		
Sundry creditor (VAT)	800	(61,800)	(3,400)
			110,100
Financed by:			
Share capital			20,000
Retained earnings			50,100
			70,100
14 per cent Debenture (repayable 1996)			40,000
			110,100

Cash flow, or lack of it, was always an item of concern to Murphy and Pat Brady, his accountant. Eastern Oil had borrowed heavily in recent years to acquire its fixed assets which included renovated premises and expanded storage facilities capable of holding up to 200,000 gallons of oil. In addition three delivery trucks were purchased for cash since hire purchase facilities were considered to be too expensive. Working capital requirements were financed exclusively by a bank overdraft which was secured on stock and debtors. Long term borrowings were secured on the remaining assets of the company.

The accountant, Pat Brady, explained that the ability of Eastern Oil to establish a reasonable, useful budget for next year was dependent on the ability to understand the market and plan their sales forecasts accordingly. The demand for oil, as everyone knew, was seasonal and the budgets had to take this seasonality factor into account. Because of this he suggested that monthly rather than quarterly budgets be prepared.

The sales manager, Tony Cox, produced a summary of monthly sales, i.e. deliveries during the twelve months just ended (Exhibit 2). The summary of monthly sales, Cox explained, related to the year ending 30 June, 1987. He added that gallons delivered for the period were double that of the previous year indicating that there was a general upward trend in sales. However there was also a considerable monthly variation in demand. During the winter months and especially around Christmas demand peaked, whereas business was very slack during the summer months.

Exhibit 2. Monthly sales (gallons) for 12 months ended 30 June 1987

Period	Month		Gallons
25	July	1986	25,000
26	August	1986	30,000
27	September	1986	40,000
28	October	1986	60,000
29	November	1986	80,000
30	December	1986	130,000
31	January	1987	110,000
32	February	1987	90,000
33	March	1987	70,000
34	April	1987	50,000
35	May	1987	40,000
36	June	1987	40,000
			765,000

In order to help in the forecasting of sales, Cox had hired marketing consultants. They analysed the sales volume for the past three years and they were able to determine a definite trendline and identify average seasonal variations. Cox tested the forecasts retrospectively and found that they were very accurate. For example, he said, that the forecast for June 1987, which was month 36, was only 100 gallons less than actual outturn. Cox then produced a summary of the statistical research findings (Exhibit 3).

Both Murphy and Brady were impressed by research of this type. After extensive discussion it was decided that this data should be used in predicting demand levels and budget forecasts for next year. The only provision was that all forecasts should be rounded *down* to the nearest

71

1,000 gallons so as to simplify the overall construction of budgetary figures.

Exhibit 3.

Trendline for oil demand: $Y = 22,400 + 1436T$
  where Y = monthly demand (in gallons)
        T = month (i.e. 25 for July 1986) etc.
        and adjusted for average monthly variations.
Average monthly variations (per centage) from trendline:

July, August, April, May, June	– 25 per cent
September, March	+ 10 per cent
October	+ 40 per cent
November, December, January	+130 per cent
February	+ 70 per cent

Brady explained that the seasonality of the oil business would impose cash flow pressures. For example, in the previous year, serious shortages occurred due to lack of supplies caused mainly by industrial disputes among road tanker drivers in the supplying company. As a result it had already been decided, from July 1987, to maintain closing stock levels equal to anticipated gallon sales for the forthcoming month. This policy although prudent would create automatically cash flow pressures on Eastern Oil, since suppliers require and receive payment on delivery. The current purchase price per gallon is eighty-eight pence inclusive of VAT at ten per cent. However, due to the nature of the business VAT was charged only on sales and purchases of oil and the company accounts for VAT on an invoice basis.

Patrick Murphy then asked about cash flow from sales, especially since volume sold would probably break the magical 1 million gallon mark during the forthcoming year. Pat Brady replied that the policy of cash on delivery applied in theory only but not in practice. One problem was that many industrial firms whom they supplied automatically took thirty days credit. It just wasn't feasible to trade with them on any other terms, he explained. Eastern Oil also supplied local schools and health board offices which were notoriously slow in paying their accounts. Brady indicated that an analysis of past sales dockets revealed the following payment pattern.

50 per cent cash on delivery
40 per cent received in month following sale
10 per cent received in second month following sale.

There was no evidence to suggest that this payment pattern would be significantly different in the forthcoming year and bad debts were not anticipated.

72

Sales deliveries were undertaken by the three tanker drivers employed by Eastern Oil. Murphy knew that having three trucks on the road at any one time was a luxury. However if Eastern Oil was to maintain its guarantee of delivery within twenty-four hours, three drivers and three trucks was an absolute minimum to have on the road at any one time. It was an expensive strategy, Murphy accepted, since it cost £21,000 in wages to keep a driver on the road for a year. A recently concluded national wage agreement which takes effect on 1 September 1987 offers them a five per cent increase per annum with an additional increase of eight per cent per annum commencing 1 April, 1988.

Remaining expenses of the company are to be grouped for budgetary purposes under the headings of depreciation of fixed assets, administration costs, delivery costs, and interest charges. Depreciation on fixed assets is provided on a straight line method at the following annual rates:

Buildings   12 per cent per annum
Vehicles   20 per cent per annum
Equipment 25 per cent per annum

Administration costs consist primarily of salaries of managers and other administrative staff. Based on current data these would amount to £60,000 per annum and would be paid on a monthly basis. Delivery costs, which included mainly diesel fuel for lorries, are budgeted at ten per cent of sales revenue and are deemed to be discharged monthly. Debenture interest is paid six monthly in arrears. Bank overdraft interest is credited to the firm's current account at the rate of ten per cent per annum. By special arrangement with the bank manager interest payable is credited at the end of each quarter based on the average opening monthly balance for each of the three months in the relevant quarter. Murphy realised that this arrangement was a generous concession obtained from the bank manager. It was negotiated some years ago when the firm's bank overdraft rarely exceeded £5,000. How things had changed! From recent discussions with his bank manager Murphy appreciated that the present arrangement might not last much longer unless the company was able to considerably improve its cash flow position during the forthcoming year.

It was Murphy's intention that the final agreed budget would become the basis for evaluating overall company performance. Actual results would be compared with budgeted amounts each month and cumulatively, and variances from the budget would be investigated and discussed. By seeking to build on realistic projections, the budget would give credibility with the bank. Thus Murphy argued that the budget should be viewed much more than a set of targets or objectives for internal purposes in that they had important implications for the company.

Murphy was confident about the budgetary control process to be introduced in his company. Even though a great deal of time and effort was needed to produce a realistic budget and monitor actual performance, it had the benefit of forcing management to think about future selling tasks and the relevant financing needs. After all these were the essential elements which would determine the overall profitability and future of the company.

REQUIREMENT

1   Prepare a forecast monthly cash budget and income statement for the year ended 30 June 1988, together with a balance sheet at that date.

2   Identify the major assumptions and issues involved in the budgeting process. What criticisms would you make of the budgetary process as described?

3   How could the company improve its cash flow and profitability performance?

Case 2.3 XT Pharmaceuticals

In May 1988 John Fleming the managing director of XT Pharmaceuticals, a manufacturing division within a large multinational company, was disappointed with his company's failure to meet forecasted sales and profits during the first four months of 1988. Currently sales for the year were running about ten per cent below forecast and the company's profit, according to preliminary statements (Exhibit 1), was also below budget. This was disappointing for Fleming since he was held entirely responsible for his company's profit performance, measured in terms of return on total assets (ROTA). Of greater significance to Fleming was the possible ramification for him personally. He was widely tipped to be promoted to head office before the end of the year. However a ROTA of anything less than fifteen per cent would seriously impair his chances of this much sought after promotion.

The budgetary process in XT pharmaceuticals typically began a few months before the start of the new financial year. The first step in the process was to prepare a detailed estimate of expected sales for the forthcoming year. These estimates were gathered from two sources: the marketing department who were responsible for the overall promotion of the firm's products and a sales manager who was responsible for actual sales. However the sales force, unlike the marketing personnel, were remunerated by way of basic salary, commission and their ability to achieve budget targets. Fleming felt that one estimate would serve as a good check on the other, and also believed that participation in setting the plan was one way to ensure its effectiveness. The marketing department group prepared their estimates by subdividing the market into two parts: sales resulting from normal industry growth at current levels of market penetration and increased sales resulting from further penetration of the market with existing products. At the same time, the sales manager, after consulting with his sales representatives, predicted the volume of orders that each customer would place in 1988.

Exhibit 1. Comparison of actual and budgeted performance, January-April 1988

	Budgeted	Actual
Sales	£2,713,000	£2,440,000
Direct labour	900,000	990,000
Direct materials	600,000	550,000
Production overhead	500,000	300,000
Marketing and selling	300,000	280,000
Administration	93,000	91,000
Research	100,000	40,000
Profit	220,000	189,000

The sales manager produced an estimate of product X sales of £3,290,000 for 1988, and the marketing department estimated sales of £3,400,000. Fleming felt that the two estimates were in reasonable agreement and incorporated the higher of the two figures into the profit plan. On the other hand, the marketing department estimated sales of product T at £4,000,000, while the sales force predicted only £3,000,000. Sales for the product had been £1,000,000 in 1986 and £2,000,000 in 1987. Fleming felt that the disparity between the two estimates was a significant one and he discussed the matter with both groups. He finally decided that the sales force had submitted a conservative estimate and agreed that the figure submitted by the marketing department was the more realistic goal.

Once the total sales estimate of £7,400,000 was decided upon by Fleming, the process of estimating production costs began. Each product is produced in separate departments under the responsibility of individual managers. The two production managers were furnished with the sales estimates and asked to forecast direct labour costs, supervisory salaries and production overhead expenses. The expenses were to be forecast monthly and were to be used subsequently as a yardstick by which the actual expenses were to be monitored and the managers to be evaluated.

The production department responsible for product X had been a problem area within the division for sometime and four department managers had resigned or been fired during the last three years. A new manager, David Ryan, had just been appointed and was informed that he was expected to have his department on budget by the end of the year. In response Ryan indicated that his new department had performed poorly in recent years. He further pointed out that he had been in charge for only two months. Fleming replied 'I'm expected to meet my profit targets. The only way that can occur is if my subordinates exercise control over their expenses and achieve their budgets.'

The manager responsible for product T responded to the budget request in prompt fashion. Since the budgeted output was exactly double that of the previous year, he doubled the appropriate budgeted costs for the previous year. He then reduced his individual cost estimates by five per cent to allow for increased efficiency.

Fleming, a pharmacist by profession, requested the purchasing department to estimate direct material cost for each product based on quantities required. Since the purchasing manager thought that it was impossible to predict what all the raw material prices would be, he increased last year's standard prices by ten per cent. The marketing, administration and research departments forecast their own expenses. Due to Fleming's inexperience in these areas, these estimates were accepted largely without discussion.

With the various forecasts in hand, the accounts department

estimated a profit of £600,000 for the year, based on a sales volume of £7,400,000. Once this draft profit figure had been drawn up, it was reviewed by Fleming in relation to the specific profit and sales goals required by head office for his company. In reviewing the plans of each department, it became obvious that the combined plans of the company were not sufficient to meet the overall required target. Fleming confirmed his suspicion by consulting the firm's financial prosition at 31 December 1987 (Exhibit 2).

Exhibit 2. Balance sheet at 31 December 1987

Fixed assets at cost	£3,900,000	
Less: aggregate depreciation......................	(2,100,000)	£1,800,000
Current assets		
Stock	1,400,000	
Debtors	500,000	
Bank balances	400,000	
	2,300,000	
Less: Current liabilities		
Creditors	(1,300,000)	1,000,000
		2,800,000

Based on his budgeted ROTA, the planned sales volume for XT Pharmaceuticals was therefore revised by Fleming upward by ten per cent to £8,140,000 and profit to £660,000. Fleming thought that this was a difficult but achievable plan and one that would satisfy head office.

By mid May Fleming was very concerned about the poor profit performance of his division relative to budget and contemplated three alternatives to improve the situation. First, he was considering the elimination of £30,000 from the advertising budget for the remainder of 1988, but had not discussed it with the marketing department. Second, he thought of postponing the addition of two research scientists to his staff until next year. He had made plans to hire two research personnel by the middle of the current year. one of whom would investigate certain production processes which were yielding excessive labour inefficiency variances. The other would research and ultimately develop new products. Fleming estimated that postponing the hiring of these men would save £35,000 in salaries and supporting expenses. Finally, Fleming was thinking about reducing raw material purchases in order to reduce investment in stocks and thus improve his company's return on total assets. The reduction in stock levels was an attractive possibility since stocks accounted for almost thirty five per cent of total assets. He recognised, however, that this course of action involved risks.

Fleming realised that top management in head office would not be satisfied with his explanations of failure to meet plans. The message, though not stated explicity, seemed to be that he was expected to take whatever remedial and alternative courses of action were needed in order to meet the one-year goals. He was certain that real pressure was building up for him and his managers to meet targets.

REQUIREMENT

1   What is the budgeted ROTA and what is it likely to be for the year? How appropriate is it in evaluating the performance of an autonomous division? Explain.

2   Critically examine the budget practices described. What are the possible effects on David Ryan if the present method of budget administration is continued?

3   What are the immediate and long-term effects of the three alternatives which Fleming is considering?

Case 2.4 The Kelly Company

In July 1987, Bernard Daly was appointed managing director of the Kelly Company. Daly had been employed in the company for five years and had previous responsibility for production and quality control. He readily admits his shortcomings in the areas of accounting and finance but, being married to the chairman's daughter, he knew that other board members would readily cooperate with him.

The Kelly Company produces a well-known consumer product in three different varieties: Standard, Special and Deluxe. Although these products were household names, with a large degree of customer loyalty, the company's profit levels have been unacceptably low in recent years. Daly attributed this lack of profitability to poor production and product planning and even worse cost control and communication. Monthly head of department meetings were confined to the winter months only so as not to encroach on the golfing season. When they did take place there was little enthusiasm for real analysis of discussion, partly because of the lack of accounting information.

On taking up his new post, Daly had a series of meetings with his chief accountant in which the topic of discussion was the need for a new financial planning and control system within the company. The outcome of these private discussions was the determination to improve

Exhibit 1. Stock availability and input requirements per product

DIRECT MATERIALS

Material type	Standard	Special	Deluxe	Cost	Opening Stock (valued at std.)
		lbs. per unit			
No. 101	1	1	2	£1 lb.	4,000 lbs.
No. 102	2	3	4	£1.20 lb.	6,000 lbs.
No. 103	nil	3	5	50p lb.	3,500 lbs.

The only production constraint is the availability of material type No. 102, the supply of which is restricted to 18,000 lbs. per month in the forthcoming year.

DIRECT LABOUR INPUT

Each product must pass through two different production processes. Each unit requires the exact same labour time so that unit labour cost of all three products are identical. The relevant data are:

PROCESS	Direct labour time per finished unit	Hourly rate
Assembly	10 mins.	£12
Finishing	20 mins.	£15

company profitability through better production planning, setting more realistic selling prices and to ensure strict monitoring and control over major cost items by the introduction of a standard costing system based on marginal rather than on absorption costing principles.

The chief accountant, John Brennan, was entrusted with the task of preparing monthly budgets for the forthcoming year ending June 1988 which he would present to a specially convened meeting of all department heads. It was agreed that a standard variable costing system would be more appropriate for planning and control purposes than an absorption system. Initially Brennan collected information relating to all three products produced by the firm (Exhibit 1).

As always, information of production overheads was difficult to obtain. Brennan, after discussing the matter with Daly, decided to absorb the overheads on the basis of total direct labour hours. As yet, the precise relationship between production overheads and direct labour hours had to be determined but Brennan was able to obtain the following details for a recent ten-month period (Exhibit 2); the data for November and December were unavailable. Brennan thought that this data would be suitable for prediction purposes using regression analysis.

Exhibit 2*.

	Total direct labour hours	Total production overhead (excluding depreciation)
Jan	1,500	£800
Feb	2,000	1,000
Mar	3,000	1,350
April	2,500	1,250
May	3,000	1,300
June	2,500	1,200
July	3,500	1,400
Aug	3,000	1,250
Sept	2,500	1,150
Oct	1,500	800
	25,000	11,500

Note: See Exhibit 4 for results of simple regression analysis.

The remaining expenses consist mainly of administration and selling expenses. Administration expenses amount to £24,000 per annum, largely due to the small numbers of office staff. Selling expenses consist of a monthly advertising outlay of £2,000.

Having obtained all the relevant costing information Brennan looked at possible selling prices for the products. Selling prices established in previous years, by way of mark-up on cost, had been unsatisfactory. Daly had agreed that selling prices be determined as follows:

Standard: fifty per cent mark up on unit variable cost;
Special: to provide a contribution/sales ratio of fifty per cent;
Deluxe: unit variable cost plus £14

and that the maximum sales for each product would be restricted to 3,000 units.

Based on the above information which he gathered, Brennan prepared an optimal production plan for the first month of the new financial year, assuming profit maximisation, together with various operating expense standards and budgets, profit and cash flow projections. Having surveyed his work Brennan was satisfied that his projections were the proper basis for establishing a budgetary control system.

However at the end of the first month, Brennan noticed many variances from budget.

The actual results for the month of July 1987 are summarised in Exhibit 3.

Exhibit 3. Summary of actual performance for July 1987

1. Materials

	Purchased	Closing stock
Part 101	8,000 lbs at £1.10 each	1,000 lbs
Part 102	18,000 lbs at £1.30 each	1,000 lbs
Part 103	21,000 lbs at 50p each	nil

2. Direct labour
Direct labour hours worked during the month were as follows:

Assembly	900 hours	= £11,700
Finishing	2,000 hours	= £28,000

3. Other expenses
Other expenses incurred during the month were:

Variable production overhead	£600
Fixed production overhead	400
Administration expenses	3,000
Selling expenses	3,000
	7,000

4. Production
During the month the following quantities were produced and sold:

Standard	1,800 units
Special	2,100 units
Deluxe	2,400 units

5. Stocks
There was no work in progress at the start or end of the month.

Exhibit 4.

Using simple regression analysis the following results were obtained based on ten monthly observations:

Independent variable (x)   Total direct labour hours
Dependent variable (y)   Total production overhead

Coefficient of correlation (R) 0.97
Coefficient of determination. (R^2) 0.94

Coefficients of the regression equation:
    Intercept or constant .... 368, i.e. £368
    Independent variable 0.32
    Standard error of the regression coefficient for the
    independent variable 0.028
    t-value for a 95 per cent confidence interval (10 degrees
    of freedom) 2.228
    t-value for a 95 per cent confidence interval
    (8 degrees of freedom) 2.306
    Durbin-Watson statistic 1.567

REQUIREMENT

1. Prepare appropriate budgets for July 1987 which would form the basis of budgetary control in the Kelly company.

2. Analyse cost and revenue variances between budget and actual for July 1987 and use them to reconcile actual with budget profit for the month. Comment on your calculations.

Case 2.5 Ross Shirts

Ross McMahon is the owner and general manager of Ross Shirts, a small but rapidly growing manufacturer of long-sleeved, body-fit shirts which are sold mainly under contract to large department stores.

Ross Shirts was founded ten years ago by the late Paul McMahon to produce a variety of textile items, including a large range of male and female clothing. It had stayed at a relatively modest size, in spite of a growing reputation for quality. When Paul McMahon started the company it was sufficiently small for him to personally supervise all operations. As a result an elaborate cost accounting system was considered neither necessary or appropriate. Paul McMahon paid himself and his employees 'generous remuneration' and as long as his overdraft was below agreed limits, he was satisfied with his firm's progress.

The untimely death of its founder had brought the firm to virtual collapse twelve months ago. When Ross inherited his father's business he immediately launched a rationalisation plan. He eliminated the ladies range of items since the profit margin and overall labour efficiency in that area were low. Many staff were made redundant although some were re-engaged on a strictly contract basis. Production was initially concentrated on the mensware range and now all production facilities was devoted to shirt manufacturing. It was anticipated that this rationalisation would eliminate unnecessary overheads and allow the company to benefit from the increased productivity of the work force.

McMahon also realised that he needed a really good cost accounting system since textile manufacturing was a low-margin business due to intense competition for the large department store trade. For small manufacturers such as Ross Shirts selling prices were largely determined by competition. Ross appreciated therefore that the overall profitability of his manufacturing operation depended on his ability to control and monitor all costs, production and otherwise. Ross recently hired an accountant, Alan King, to design and install a new management accounting and information system. King was given the title of company accountant and given full responsibility for all accounting functions. Within a short space of time King had installed a temporary budgetary control system based on a monthly reporting cycle.

King's first step in developing a reporting system for costs was to establish a standard quantity of material used for each batch of 1,000 dozen shirts. This information was supplied by production personnel with good working knowledge of the materials used in the production process. These physical quantities were then priced at standard prices supplied by the purchasing department. The same procedure was adopted in relation to production labour expect that in this case labour rate data was obtained from the personnel department. The standard direct labour input was based on performance data collected by production personnel during a recent test month. The test month had revealed large adverse variances in virtually all cost and revenue items. In discussing the performance report, McMahon accepted that many of the original standards were 'too tight' and it was agreed to revise them. The revised and agreed standard costs for December — the last month of the calendar year — are set out in Exhibit 1. The selling price per dozen was set so as to provide a thirty-three and one-third per cent margin on sales.

Exhibit 1. Standard cost shirt for one dozen mens' shirts

Direct materials (24 yards @ 0.75p)	£18.00
Direct labour (2 hours @ £10)	20.00
Factory overhead (£18 per standard direct labour hour)*	36.00
Administration overhead	6.00
	£80.00

*The budgeted volume for the month, based on normal production, was 2,900 dozen shirts (or 5,800 direct labour hours). The budgeted amount of fixed overhead at normal production volume was £58,000.

King acknowledges that his newly installed management accounting information system is still imperfect. Its principal merit is that it is simple to operate and its implementation did not require any significant change in current work practices. King believes that once the system is accepted he can gradually improve it with the co-operation of senior staff members.

Under the budgetary control system the purchasing manager was given full responsibility for purchasing the correct material at the budgeted price or as near as was feasible. Because of this newly imposed responsibility it was anticipated that material price variances would not be significant and so, King maintained all stocks at standard cost in the nominal ledger. The standard cost of the items purchased are entered in the nominal ledger whenever materials are received. However issues of materials to production are not recorded as they are issued due to the absence of a regular storekeeper. Rather a complete stock take is carried out at the end of each month. Subtracting the closing stock balance from opening stock plus purchases for the month provides a measure of actual usage for the month. Any excess usage of raw materials was the responsibility of the production manager. The monthly stock take includes a check on closing work in progress.

In relation to production labour all employees are paid the same basic hourly rate. The hours worked are obtained from the weekly clock cards punched by each employee. This ensures that direct labour cost is recorded on an accrual rather than a cheque payment basis. Overtime is a rare occurrence and King has insisted that any overtime must first be sanctioned by him before it is undertaken. The hours worked are then compared with the standard direct labour hours of the work done and a variance is reported at the end of each month.

Production overheads comprise general factory overhead and also materials such as buttons and thread which are classified as overheads for convenience purposes. Overheads are accumulated on an invoice received basis or usage basis, whichever King considers to be more accurate. At the end of the month when closing work in progress is priced at standard, a transfer is made from work in progress account to finished goods account to reflect the standard cost of the goods completed. Likewise an adjusting entry is made to the cost of goods sold account to reflect the cost of goods actually sold during the period. The system is designed so that the balances in all stock accounts represent the standard costs of all stock in hand at the end of the reporting period. As King remarked to McMahon, 'It sure simplifies our stock valuation procedures.' However McMahon queried, 'Will our auditors accept it?'

It was a penetrating question and King didn't know the answer since he had not prepared the accounts for the month of December. As a result he didn't know whether his variances would be significant or not. Hopefully they would not be significant since he could then write them off to his income statement for the period. However if they were considered material by the auditor then he would be required to rework his closing stock valuations. The opening balances in the various ledger accounts at 1 December (Exhibit 2) and the summary of operations for December (Exhibit 3) had just been delivered into his office.

Exhibit 2. Opening balances in selected ledger accounts

Raw materials (40,000 yards @ £0.75p)	£30,000
Finished goods	74,000
Work in progress	nil
Accounts payable	46,000
Accounts receivable	39,000
Bank overdraft	2,000
Shareholders funds	95,000

REQUIREMENT

1 Prepare an income statement based on the above data for the month of December under the assumption that a standard absorption costing system is employed.

2 Reconcile your income statement with budget for month using detailed variances on individual cost items and revenue. Suggest possible reasons for all variances calculated and indicate what persons would ordinarily be held responsible for them.

Exhibit 3. Summary of operations: December

1. Total material purchases for month, 95,000 yards at a cost of £72,200.
2. 5,500 hours of direct labour were registered on clock cards at a cost of £51,000.
3. Factory overhead incurred amounted to £110,000 of which sixty per cent was considered fixed.
4. Administrative overhead incurred, £17,000.
5. Payments to accounts payable amounted to £220,000 (including expenses payable).
6. 3,100 dozen shirts were sold on account for £121 per dozen.
7. Closing stock of raw materials amounted to 66,000 yards.
8. Cash receipts from customers amounted to £390,000.
9. Closing stock of finished goods amounted to 900 dozen shirts.

3 To what extent does the new system meet the needs of management? What changes would you consider bearing in mind the additional costs to be incurred on their implementation?

4 How would you dispose of the standard cost variances for year-end financial accounting purposes? Defend your calculations.

5 To what extent does the division of responsibility for purchasing and use of materials create additional problems? Explain.

Case 2.6 Magee Electronics

'Are you absolutely sure your figures are correct?' queried John Magee with an air of desperation in his voice.

The reply was confident and positive. 'I've doubled-checked them. John, you've got to accept the fact that my figures are correct and that we are way over budget for the quarter.'

John Magee, major shareholder and managing director of Magee Electronics had just spoken on the phone with his accountant, Simon O'Leary. The topic of conversation was the operating performance of the company for the first quarter just ended (Exhibit 1). Magee found it difficult to follow the layout of the report but the message was nevertheless clear: labour costs and variable overheads were out of control but there was no apparent explanation — just significant adverse cost variances.

Magee Electronics manufactures a variety of electronic devices for export to its American parent company. As a result of anticipated slack production capacity during the forthcoming year Magee was persuaded to manufacture special electronic control devices for a producer of automated assembly lines.

A major factor influencing Magee's decision to take on this special order for 4,000 units was that an associated company had produced the same quantity of similar control devices for the same customer the previous year. In fact it was the associated company's inability to continue the contract which resulted in Magee Electronics being approached. Magee was assured that the special control devices basically involved an assembly operation, which required a degree of skill and the average time taken would be five hours per unit for 4,000 units. Magee was happy to rely on this information regarding labour input.

In order to prepare a budget for this special order Magee consulted his accountant, Simon O'Leary. Prior to joining the firm, O'Leary obtained a business studies degree at University. He had intended to subsequently pursue a formal accountancy qualification but never got round to it. As he explained about himself, 'his best intentions got highjacked.' Nevertheless O'Leary's work was always competent especially when it came to credit control and submitting PAYE and VAT returns.

O'Leary and Magee, after some discussion agreed the following standard marginal cost for each special control device (Exhibit 2). Magee was happy regarding the standard for labour input. O'Leary felt that the standards for both materials and variable overhead were reasonable.

Three months later Magee did not know where to start looking for the cause of the adverse operating variances. O'Leary suggested that the original standards were incorrect especially in relation to labour hours

Exhibit 1. Summary of performance for January-March (special control devices)

	Jan	Feb	Mar	Total
Actual sales units	300	340	350	990
Actual sales units at £130 each	£39,000	£44,200	£45,500	£128,700
Output data:				
Planned production	315	335	335	985
Actual production	300	340	350	990
Materials purchased (units)	2,000	1,200	1,300	4,500
Total cost and materials	£20,200	£12,120	£13,260	£45,580
Materials used (units)	1,300	1,300	1,400	4,000
Labour hours worked (hours)	3,453	2,440	1,866	7,759
Labour cost	£21,000	£15,000	£12,000	£48,000
Variable overhead incurred	£3,500	£2,500	£2,000	£8,000
Fixed overhead incurred	£4,000	£3,400	£3,800	£11,200

Summary (Jan–March)	Budget (985 units)	Actual (990 units)	Variance	
Sales	£128,050	£128,700	+£650	0.5%
Materials purchased	39,400	45,580	(6,180)	15.7%
Labour cost	29,550	48,000	(18,450)	62.4%
Variable overhead	4,925	8,000	(3,075)	62.4%
Fixed overhead	10,500	11,200	(700)	6.6%

Exhibit 2. Standard variable manufacturing cost

Materials (4 units at £10 each)	40.00
Assembly labour (5 hours at £6 each)	30.00
Variable overhead (5 hours at £1 each)	5.00
	75.00

which in turn affected variable overheads. Magee thought that to accept that planning variances were the cause of the adverse operating performance was the easy way out. The problem, Magee felt, lay on the operational and not on the planning side. In addition, Magee pondered how one could explain the fact that things seemed to be improving. Labour costs, he noted, were significantly down in March compared with February, even though production was slightly increased. Moreover Magee had again confirmed with the manager of the associated company that their average time taken to produce the 4,000 units last year was five hours. Magee knew that the manufacturing operations in both companies were similar and both companies had a workforce with equal capabilities. No, Magee was confident that an average of five hours per unit was the correct standard to use. 'But I wonder will our results ever match standard in the future', he asked himself.

His thoughts were interrupted by a knock on the door and the sudden presence in his office of his daughter, Susan. It was time to go home. Magee didn't realise that it was so late. 'Hi, dad! How are things?'

'It's good to see you,' replied Magee, being polite but very sincere. 'To be frank,' he added, 'things are not going so well with one of our operations; well over budget and I don't know why.'

'Show me,' responded Susan with a genuine sound of curiosity in her voice. Susan was a bright accounting student at college so Magee willingly complied with her request.

Susan studied the two exhibits for a while, Magee rose from his chair to get his coat. 'Ah, yes,' she exclaimed, 'I think I know what may be your problem. Did you ever hear of the learning curve effect that occurs with increased production?'

Magee sat down again.

'All I need is a calculator with a log function and some peace and quiet, to test my learning curve hypothesis. I believe I might be able to explain everything to you.'

'I'll make the coffee,' responded Magee.

REQUIREMENT

1. Is Susan correct in thinking that a learning curve effect is present in the above production operation? Explain.

2. Based on your analysis in requirement 1 above, prepare a revised budget for the months of January, February and March. Calculate appropriate standard cost variances. The company operates a standard marginal costing system.

3. Calculate the overall profit/loss on the contract, assuming 4,000 units are produced. Explain your figures.

4. Discuss the implications of the learning curve for managerial planning and control techniques.

Case 2.7 Palmer Productions

Tom Palmer was a little confused with the recently installed financial planning and budgetary control system in his factory. Palmer Productions manufactures a single product which is sold directly to consumers. Since the product was considered to be extremely price sensitive Palmer recognised that proper selling price determination and cost control would be the major determinants of profitability in his company. To this end he had employed a consultant to advise on modern pricing techniques and an adequate costing system.

The consultant recommended a switch to the economic approach to pricing policy since this would allow the company to maximise its profits. Previously the company had determined its selling price by adding a specific mark-up to cost. After extensive research the consultant was able to determine the firm's demand curve for its product. The demand curve had since been used to determine an optimal selling price for the firm's product and is specified as follows:

$$P = 65 - .0005 \, X$$
where: P = selling price,
X = quantity demanded

Palmer was initially sceptical that economic theory could have any relevance to business management. However the results of economic pricing had been most satisfactory and company profitability had rapidly improved.

Simultaneously the consultant helped install a 'management by exception' reporting system to assist management identify the major cost variances and therefore the areas most likely to benefit from investigation. Palmer anticipated that significant cost variances should be a rare occurrence because he had a well-trained labour force and manufacturing operations were well structured. His accounting department had produced the following estimates of total costs for various levels of output as follows:

Number of units	Total cost of production
40,000	£800,000
50,000	£950,000
60,000	£1,100,000

While Palmer appreciated the concept of management by exception he also realised that any subsequent investigation of variances was a costly process. The cost of investigation amounted to £10,000 mainly due to lost production, or alternatively, working overtime to compensate for lost hours. On the other hand, the cost of correction, if applicable, was zero. However, previous cost investigations sometimes indicated variances caused largely by normal or random variations in operating conditions. Thus the company had incurred a cost of investigation without any corresponding benefit. On the other hand failure to investigate a cost variance could result in failure to identify and correct inefficiencies. Thus savings on failure to investigate would be outweighed by the loss due to continuing inefficiencies. Palmer felt that he would have to decide on a variance investigation strategy that would incorporate the costs of investigation, possible benefits due to correction and the profitability that the operating system was in need of correction. At present Palmer investigated all unfavourable cost variances but he realised that his present investigation policy was a potential waste of his time and company resources.

Before Palmer decided on a cost variance investigation strategy he received his exception report indicating that the variable cost of production had increased by £5 for the last month. As usual, he was unsure as to the cause of this significant variance. Based on previous experience he felt that there was only a twenty per cent chance that it was a random variation and therefore non-correctable and so would not occur in the following month. In such case current pricing strategy, based on marginal cost, would remain unchanged. On the other hand, Palmer realised that the variance could be caused by inefficient operations which would continue for the next month until corrected. Alternatively the cost increase could represent a permanent or non-correctable change. Palmer assigned these latter explanations equal probability. If the change in cost was permanent then Palmer felt that standard costs should be revised and his best strategy would be to adapt to the increased cost by changing current selling prices. If the cause was due to production inefficiencies then investigation was advisable.

Due to time pressures generated by other commitments Palmer was tempted not to investigate the recent cost variance. Rather he could retain or adjust his selling price and calculate the best price to be charged on the basis of expected value. It was a fairly simple calculation, thought Palmer. His only two strategies in relation to selling price were to retain his current selling price or adjust it. Each strategy was associated with uncertainty regarding whether the variance was random, permanent or could be corrected. The decision to investigate was thus a complex one for Palmer. He knew the costs of investigating any variance was £10,000. He also knew that the 'value' of the investigation decision revolved around the possible discovery and correction of possible inefficiencies in manufacturing operations, but another part would be due to the investigation's aid in deciding on the appropriate selling price if the increased variable cost was considered permanent.

91

REQUIREMENT

1 Construct a pay-off table for Palmer, in terms of contribution, reflecting his own pricing strategies if he does not investigate.

2. Would you recommend investigation? Why?

3 What is the maximum amount that Palmer would be willing to pay for perfect information on the cause of the variance? Explain your figures.

Case 2.8 National Products Group

The National Products Group manufactures furniture and consists of two autonomous branches. The creation of two separate branches was the product of history and geographical location rather than commercial logic. Each branch is treated as a separate profit centre and the manager's ability to generate profits is the key factor in determining his remuneration. Each manager is responsible for the sales of his branch and had virtually complete discretion over the method of sales promotion to be used and customer selection. In recent years each branch has concentrated on the manufacture of a relatively limited range of models designed to serve different markets in the furniture industry. Because the markets and products of each branch are so different, there have never been any transfers between them.

The Athy branch of National Products manufactures furniture that is used for catering purposes. Its principal products are strong, rectangular tables and hard-backed chairs which are sold mainly to large institutions. Typical clients include universities and regional colleges who require robust furniture for their canteens. The standard direct cost of production are contained in Exhibit 1.

Exhibit 1. Athy branch: standard direct costs

	Table	Set of chairs (each)
Raw materials	£41.00	£20.00
Direct labour		
Cutting	10.00	10.00
Assembly	10.00	10.00
	61.00	40.00

Direct labour is paid at the rate of £10 per hour. In addition overhead is charged to each product on the basis of machine hours. The estimates of production overhead and machine hours for both departments for the forthcoming year are contained in Exhibit 2.

The Athy branch operates a full cost pricing policy. The mark-up on total production cost is fifty per cent for each product and this policy, in previous years, has produced satisfactory profit performances. It is not intended to change this policy next year, since the Athy branch is projected to operate at maximum capacity, defined as 5,000 hours in the cutting department. This is the only constraint under which the Athy branch will operate under next year.

The Sligo branch produces a totally different range of furniture products but is predicted to operate at only sixty per cent capacity next year. Many of its employees will be on short working time and employed

93

Exhibit 2. Overhead and recovery rates for cutting and assembly departments (Athy branch)

	Cutting	Assembly
Fixed overhead	£18,000	£10,000
Variable overhead	36,000	20,000
Total overhead	54,000	30,000
Machine hours	9,000	5,000
Absorption rate per machine hour	£6	£6
Machine hours required per table	1 hour	0.5 hours
Machine hours required per chair	0.5 hours	0.5 hours

on a daily basis. However, Sligo branch's administrative and other support staff have not been cut.

Frank Ferris, Sligo's manager, is actively seeking profitable ways to utilise his branch's idle capacity during the forthcoming year. One day, last week he was studying some reports prepared by his firm's sales department. Ferris had been considering for some time the possibility of producing cheap office desks which would be a considerably 'stripped-down' version of the executive desk produced by other manufacturers. The sales department were confident that there was an adequate demand for such desks if priced at £170 each. Apparently this basic desk would be purchased by those individuals who wanted a desk in the home and who were either unwilling or unable to purchase the more expensive and luxurious varieties.

Ferris was pleased with the predictions of his sales staff and instructed his production manager to determine the costs that would be involved in producing a basic style desk. The plan involved purchasing the completed tables from the Athy branch, slightly modifying them to include drawers, adding a thin veneer and a varnished finish. The entire production process was very simple and the Sligo branch had the expertise and necessary production capacity available. The estimated cost of producing the basic unit is provided in Exhibit 3.

Exhibit 3.

Proposed transfer price of tables (subject to approval of Athy branch)	£90
Additional direct materials	40
Additional direct labour	20
Total overhead	4
Standard cost	154
Add: profit margin	16
Sales price of basic style desk	170

Sligo labour is paid £10 per hour and the overhead rate of £4 per unit is considered fifty per cent variable. Sligo's total fixed overheads and administrative costs are unlikely to increase as a result of producing the basic desk model but Ferris believes any business it takes on should cover its fair share of the division's costs.

When Ferris raised his proposal with his opposite number in the Athy branch, Jonathan Dixon, it was apparent that the transfer price was a matter of disagreement. The following conversation took place.

Frank Ferris:

'Jonathan, if we can get your tables, we can make the necessary modifications very easily. All we need to do is add a few simple drawers and revarnish the whole unit and we've got the ideal desk for use in the home; cheap but effective.'

Jonathan Dixon:

'I'm not at all happy about this transfer price. After all why should I sell to you at £90 when I can get a significantly higher price for my tables from my regular customers? I'm being evaluated on the basis of profitability so it doesn't make sense for me to deliberately lower my profits. In any event, unlike yourself, I don't have spare plant. I've already committed myself to producing 2,000 sets of chairs next year and I expect to operate at maximum capacity.'

Frank Ferris:

'Take a long-term view of things, John. If you sell to me cheap, I can sell cheap and this gives me the opportunity to penetrate a new market with promise of substantial future growth. If you accept this transfer price, you're getting a good mark-up on cost compared with my mark-up of ten per cent. Take a long-term view of things! Heaven only knows what will happen to the existing selling price or demand for your tables. I know the going rate is high but who knows what the price will be in the near future.'

Jonathan Dixon:

'I appreciate your point, Frank. But look at things from my point of view. The fundamental fact is that I can maximise my profits and my own remuneration next year by selling all my output to my regular customers. It would be silly of me to transfer products internally to you when there are more profitable external opportunities available. Can you not find an alternative supplier?'

Frank Ferris:

'I have made enquiries and the going rate would make my proposal unattractive. My profit margin would disappear. Besides, the guarantee of supply and its quality is questionable. I guess I've got to trade with you or not at all. Maybe we should talk to head office to see if they can give us any guidance.'

REQUIREMENT

1 Discuss the transfer price problem between the Athy and Sligo branches.

2 Given the current pricing structure, what production plan maximises the profits of the Athy branch for next year, considering the maximum availability of 5,000 machine hours in the assembly department? Do you anticipate any problems with this plan? Explain.

3 Given the current pricing structure, what production plan maximises the profits of the National Products Group?

4 What range of transfer prices might be acceptable to the two managers in order to achieve the group's profit-maximisation plan? Explain your answer.

Part 3

Cost accumulation, apportionment, allocation and absorption

Case 3.1 Metallic Products Limited

In a fortnight's time, Tony Ryan is due to join Metallic Products Limited as company accountant. The managing director, Paddy Phelan, has asked him to visit the factory for a preliminary briefing on the company's situation. The company manufactures high quality metal casings for the audio equipment market. The company has enjoyed rapid expansion with sales mainly to the UK and currently employs fifty-five persons. The factory is located on a relatively new industrial estate and Tony has no difficulty finding a parking space near the reception area. Within minutes he is being shown into Paddy Phelan's plush office and, after preliminary greetings and the arrival of coffee, Paddy gets down to business.

Paddy Phelan:
'I asked you here today, Tony, to introduce you to the rest of the management team. As you probably know we manufacture metal boxes or casings which hold the electronic circuitry in audio equipment, mainly stereos. We are therefore sheet metal workers producing metal boxes for the audio equipment industry. Quality is of the upmost importance since the metal casings must be engineered precisely to the manufacturers' specifications or else they will not take the circuitry, dials and other components of the audio equipment.'

Tony Ryan:
'How do the manufacturers specify exactly what they want?'

Paddy Phelan:
'Let me run you through a typical scenario of a customer tender. That should answer some questions and highlight some of the problems we experience. It all starts with a marketing man in a customer company. He thinks their audio equipment will sell better if they, for example, change the size of their stereos which automatically changes the size of the metal boxes for the electronic circuitry. These modifications are passed on to their design office staff who produce drawings and specifications for the metal boxes. At this stage the drawings and specifications are sent out to companies like ours with a request for a quotation. Our estimator, Con White, with help from the engineering department determines material and labour costs for the units under tender. A fixed margin is added to cover overheads and profit and Con eventually submits our estimate to the customer after liaising with our sales department. If our tender is successful, we receive a fixed price order with required delivery within a specified time. The estimating is crucial as we must stick to our estimate once given.

Tony Ryan:
'How do the estimates match up with actual costs?'

Paddy Phelan:
'Ah, that's an area I'd like you to look into closely. When we moved into this new building eighteen months ago we wanted to introduce a better accounting system to capture information from the shopfloor, so that standard labour hours could be updated and better data on material costs could be obtained. However, the system doesn't seem to have worked as well as it might. One of the problems is that different design specifications for each job can effect production time and material costs. For example, by reducing the space available for the circuitry the customer company is forcing a high degree of precision and complexity into the units to be produced. As you will appreciate one of the principal problems associated with estimating is identifying how long a job will take to pass through a work centre. Anyway you will find out more about that later. Come with me and I will introduce you to the rest of the team. I've asked each of them to spend some time with you discussing their own areas. I believe in everyone knowing what everyone else is doing. It helps communications and improves efficiency.'

At this point they left the office to meet Tony's future colleagues. Tom Devlin, the production manager, took Tony for a tour of the shopfloor. They strolled along the central aisle as Tom described the various processes involved in manufacturing operations. Tony couldn't but help notice the cluttered conditions in some work areas such as welding and packing. When he enquired about this Tom told him, 'stores are always short of parts, paint, or packing materials. Jobs are always having to be set aside until the required parts or information leaflets are delivered.' Devlin continued, 'Another problem is Frank Bradley, our sales manager. He's forever charging down here and rushing through his priority orders. This leaves other work by the wayside.' Tony wondered how this fitted into production scheduling as he knew it. His thoughts were interupted by the appearance of a casually dressed Frank Bradley.

Frank Bradley:
'Welcome to Metallic Products, Tony. Now, what can I tell you?'

Tony Ryan:
'How about filling me in on the customer profile?'

Frank Bradley:
Customers, yes, we supply to most of the big names in the business, based mainly in the UK. The market is competitive and we must therefore keep our prices keen and our performance high.'

Tony Ryan:
'How are we doing in regard to sales?'

Frank Bradley:

'Up to six months ago I would have said fine. Now, I'm not so sure. Our delivery record has been getting worse and our customers are beginning to complain and refuse to accept delivery. What's more Con White, he's the estimator, doesn't seem to realise how competitive the market is. He keeps producing quotes that make it a bit harder than it used to be to get orders. I nearly always have to reduce his figures before making a final quotation. Frank went on to draw a picture of potential disaster in the near future and complained about production being inefficient and disorganised, quality control failing too much of the subcontracted processing, and stores nearly always being short of parts.

As Tony left Frank's office he was wondering what he was letting himself in for.

It was harder to get time with John Byrne, the purchasing manager. He was making phone calls to suppliers. After Tony had been standing around for about five minutes John put the phone down.

John Bryne:

'Sorry to keep you waiting, Tony.'

The phone rang.

'Let's get to the canteen for a cup of coffee and a chat. If we stay here we'll get no peace with the boys chasing me over parts. They always want things yesterday!'

In the canteen John outlined the work of his department.

'I'm responsible for purchasing and maintaining stores. In relation to the various raw materials we classify them as follows with each group having its own coding system:

— sheet metal;
— packing and printed materials including fasteners and carboard boxes;
— miscellaneous;
— sub-contracted services;
— single piece parts including nuts and bolts for metal boxes.

We keep printed matter and packaging material in the store next to the welding area. There is a lot of heat in that area and as a result we don't have any damp problems. Everything else is in the large, main store at the other end of the factory. Our stock records are kept on a cardex system. However because of the nature of our business and occasional lack of communication production staff are constantly coming into the stores area and taking parts for production without signing for them. This makes the maintenance of accurate records very difficult.'

Tony Ryan:

'What sort of processes are sub-contracted?'

John Byrne:

'Plating. We don't have plating facilities and some design specifications require the metal casings to be specially plated. We send it out to Metal Finishers Limited, ten miles away. They're usually very quick, but recently they obtained a few big jobs and their delivery lead time to us is suffering.'

The estimator, Con White and engineering manager, Pat Orr met Tony at the same time. They work closely together in drawing up labour and material estimates for quotes. The engineering department provides both a breakdown of the product's components required for each job (bill of materials) and a description of the work to be performed (routing slip). Con White applies standard costs for material and labour to each product to give an estimate of direct cost. Estimated costs are increased by ten per cent to cover production and other overheads and a further fifteen per cent is added as a profit margin. These figures are then discussed with the sales department. Frank Bradley, the sales manager, has authority to reduce these figures before forwarding the estimate to the customer as a final and non-negotiable tender.

Before leaving Ryan paid a courtesy visit to Paddy Phelan. Both agreed that there was much need and scope for improvement in the company's accounting and information system.

Paddy Phelan:

'I think you should have a pretty good overview of what's happening here. Draft a report for discussion based on your initial observations as to how things can and should change. I don't know a lot about accounting matters so be brief and succinct — a sort of mini action plan. Feel free to raise any matter. The following documents may be of some assistance to you:

1. standard costing procedure (Exhibit 1);
2. invoicing procedure (Exhibit 2);
3. organisation structure (Exhibit 3);
4. summarised profit and loss accounts (Exhibit 4).'

REQUIREMENT

1 You are required to indicate the main weaknesses and deficiencies within the organisation especially in regard to the management accounting and information system. Suggest procedures and particularly information necessary to correct the deficiencies which you have identified.

102

Exhibit 1. Standard costing procedure

Materials:

Bought in single piece parts and paint are costed at the average price paid per unit over the last financial year plus five per cent.

Sheet metal is a more complex issue. When the engineering department have decided what size sheet of metal is to be used and how it is to be cut, the cost of the sheet (calculated in the same way as for bought in single piece parts) is allocated to each piece cut in proportion to the area of metal used in it. This means that unusable metal (wastage) is automatically costed into cut pieces to be used. However metal recuts which are necessary only when the original cuts are defective are ignored for costing purposes.

Packing materials and leaflets are costed at the price charged by the suppliers. These may be specially printed for each job as specifications are rarely the same.

Sub-contracted processing is costed per unit by dividing the price charged by the number of units processed.

Labour

Each work centre has a standard rate per hour allocated to it. This is established with reference to wage rates, based on a normal level of activity consisting of a thirty-five hour working week for each operative. Every job passing through a work centre takes a certain amount of time. This is composed of a set-up time and running time. The total time is divided by the number of units in each batch and the results multiplied by the rate per hour, thus giving a work centre cost per unit produced.

<u>**Exhibit 2.**</u> Invoicing and accounting procedure

*Completed job comes into stores from the shopfloor with a jobcard. The job number and actual labour hours recorded will have been hand written on the job card.

*Stores prepare the job for shipment.

*A four-part document is raised by stores regarding job:
Copy 1 filed in stores.

Copy 2 advice note to customer is dispatched immediately.

Copy 3 proof of delivery. Goes with load to customer, where receiving officer signs it and it is then returned to be filed in the stores.

Copy 4 production control. Production files are updated to match jobs completed with job orders. Cost of materials issued is added to form by stores personnel from their records. Form goes to accounts department where special charges such as transport are noted and added and invoice is raised based on the original job order and quotation price. This form is subsequently filed and referred to again only in the event of a customer query.

Problems

Several problems arise in relation to invoicing:

1   Wrong job numbers appear on documents raised by stores so that wrong quotation prices are given on invoices.
2   Invoices include incorrect tots and extensions and incorrect recording of VAT. Trade discounts are granted inappropriately.

Sources of error

1   Incorrect job numbers and material codes appear on job cards. This is as a result of cards being lost on the shopfloor and operatives filling in new cards incorrectly since stores will not accept jobs without completed job cards. Operatives must identify material codes if stores personnel are not present when goods are being withdrawn.
2   Recording of labour hours for each job is the sole responsibility of each operative. Some hours are not recorded due to negligence or genuine error.
3   Typing errors occur since no cross checking takes place in accounts department before invoices go out.

Exhibit 3. Current organisation structure

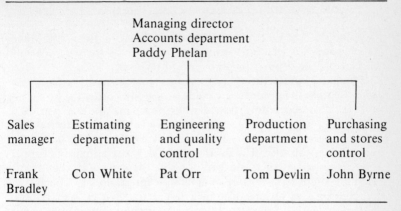

		Managing director Accounts department Paddy Phelan		
Sales manager	Estimating department	Engineering and quality control	Production department	Purchasing and stores control
Frank Bradley	Con White	Pat Orr	Tom Devlin	John Byrne

Exhibit 4. Summarised profit and loss accounts

	year ending 31.12.1987		nine months to 30.9.1988	
	£000			£000
Sales — metal boxes	4,300			3,300
Less sales returns	(400)			(330)
Net sales	3,900			2,970
Cost of sales:				
Materials	2,200		1,720	
Labour	850		650	
Overheads	300	3,350	230	2,600
Gross profit		550		370
Selling and distribution expenses		(185)		(140)
Administration expenses		(160)		(130)
Loan interest		(100)		(90)
Net profit before tax		105		10
Stock turnover (days)		80 days		90 days

Case 3.2 Reynolds Manufacturing Company

In January 1988, the three principal managers of Reynolds Manufacturing met to decide on selling price decisions for next year and the related issue of production overhead recovery.

Reynolds Manufacturing produces custom-designed kitchen furniture. Because the products are made to customer order the firm uses a job-order cost accounting system which is simple and inexpensive to operate. The company uses a single overhead absorption rate based on budgeted direct labour hours and estimated production overhead based on maximum capacity. The overhead costs consist primarily of supervision, maintenance personnel responsible for machines, repair costs including supplies, overtime premium, depreciation of machinery, building expenses such as insurance and factory power. As a result of calculating overhead recovery rates on the basis of maximum capacity, the management accounting reports always revealed a significant amount of under applied production overhead at the end of the financial year. The production manager, Joe Hickey, constantly argued that this overhead volume variance was meaningless in the context of planning or controlling production operations.

The demand for custom-made furniture, both actual and projected, was fairly constant. As a result, Tom Reynolds, owner and managing director, felt that it was appropriate to seek new production opportunities. The prospect of new orders provided the chance for Hickey to ask for a review of the current system of production overhead recovery. He had communicated his feelings to Tom Reynolds, who in turn notified the firm's accountant, Niall Leonard.

Reynolds Manufacturing recently won a contract, in the absence of local competition, to manufacture furniture for a new fast-food chain that will shortly open in the neighbourhood. In general, this furniture is extremely durable. As Tom Reynolds remarked, 'it's functional but not pretty.' Because the fast-food chain has tentative plans to expand and due to the anticipated short lifespan of the furniture, Tom Reynolds anticipates sales of the new range to grow in future years, provided, of course, selling prices could be kept reasonably low. The company has considerable spare capacity in its plant and the new product can be produced using existing facilities. In addition the industrial research department has developed an efficient manufacturing process for this furniture which does not require any additional capital investment.

For the forthcoming year both furniture products need processing in the company's two production departments. The fabricating department involves extensive use of machinery in preparing the basic material inputs. The materials are then coordinated and sent to the assembly department for assembly and packing which is labour intensive. The accounting system recognises the independence of these two production departments and charges each with the appropriate amount of direct materials and direct labour cost (excluding overtime premium). All other production costs including costs of the maintenance department are grouped as production overhead and are absorbed into production on the basis of total direct labour hours at maximum production.

The production overheads for 1988, assuming both products are produced, have been estimated by Niall Leonard on the usual basis of maximum capacity (Exhibit 1).

Exhibit 1. Estimated general production overhead for 1988

Supervisory salaries	£55,000
Maintenance wages	32,000
Maintenance supplies for machines	16,000
Production overtime premium	9,000
Straight line depreciation of machinery	36,000
Insurance and rates	14,000
Factory power	16,000
	178,000

Tom Reyonlds, being a forthright man, opened the discussion.

Tom Reynolds (Managing director):
'I've called this informal meeting to discuss overhead recovery rates for next year. I'm reasonably happy with our present system of overhead recovery. By basing our calculations on maximum capacity we get minimum unit cost and that allows us to price competitively. If we're not producing at full capacity then there is an opportunity cost involved in the form of lost profits. While our profits are satisfactory it is important to highlight the fact that they are less than what they should be. That's why I pay particular attention to the amount of our underapplied overhead.'

'I don't think the fast-food furniture units should have to bear any production overhead. Niall has suggested that most of them are fixed in nature and result from our normal production operations. If my interpretation is correct, Niall's schedule (Exhibit 1) suggests that it is not going to cost us any additional overhead to produce these extra units. Am I right, Niall?'

Niall Leonard (Accountant):
'Yes, that's right. Apart from a small increase in our variable costs which I have allowed for, you are basically correct. However, I disagree with your suggestion that the fast-food furniture shouldn't bear a portion of overheads. After all they're using the same production facilities and so should absorb their fair share of overheads.

If you don't mind me saying it you're confusing the decision to produce the units with the concept of costing them. For decision-making purposes fixed overheads are irrelevant but for pure costing purposes, for example, these fixed production overheads are important and should be taken into consideration. Certainly, our auditors will want to value the units on a full cost basis.'

Reynolds interrupted:

'Look at things from a different perspective. If I drive my car to work in the morning it costs me £2 in petrol. If I give someone a lift it still costs me £2. I'm happy with our present system but am prepared to listen to all arguments about whether we should change. If there is a better system we should consider it.'

Niall Leonard:

'There's another point that we should consider. Both products will require different processing time in the two departments. They both require roughly the same amount of labour and machine hour input in the fabricating department but the new fast-food furniture will require considerably less labour in the assembly department than our custom-made furniture, probably about half the amount. A single plantwide recovery rate for overheads means that each product is allocated a share of the overhead cost for both departments even though the time spent in each department would be different. A recovery method based on individual departments would be a more equitable way to share overheads. In addition it allows us to use different activity basis for each department.'

Joe Hickey, the production manager, who had been silent until now interjected:

'I'd like to discuss what production volume we should use for determining our overhead rates. Tom wants to use maximum capacity as in previous years but, while it gives us low unit production costs, we end up with large amounts of under-applied overhead at the end of each period. I appreciate Tom's arguments about low unit costs but ultimately I'm the person who is held responsible for these variances.'

'What do you suggest?' asked Reynolds.

Joe Hickey replied:

'I think the only proper base for overhead recovery is our expected production activity for next year. Using expected capacity we can match this year's overheads against this year's production. After all each year's costs are incurred to benefit this year's production. I would argue that each year should stand alone for recovery purposes. In that way our variances would be much more meaningful and I'm prepared to accept responsibility for them. At present because we're using maximum capacity as our base volume we end up with under-absorbed overhead. Since I'm the production manager it's pretty depressing to get the accounting reports showing large negative variances at the end of each period. Can we do anything about that Niall?'

Niall Leonard had been the accountant for Reynolds Manufacturing since the company was incorporated. His responsibility included the preparation of periodic management accounting reports which were cir-culated to managers highlighting the variances for which they were res-ponsible. He replied:

'If we are going to change our basis of activity for overhead recovery, we should opt for normal production volume. Normal production volume represents the average production volume over a period of several years. It will give a constant fixed overhead cost per unit. It will result in the under-recovery of fixed overhead in the years when actual volume is less than normal volume. Conversely, it will result in over-recovery in the years when actual volume is greater than normal volume. My point is that fixed production costs in particular should be viewed not in the context of a single year but rather over a much longer period of time.'

Tom Reynolds:
'Do we have any data which would help us in our calculations?'

Niall Leonard:
'I have a lot of data here (Exhibits 2 and 3) which I prepared for the

Exhibit 2. Miscellaneous operating data for 1988

	Fabrications Department	Assembly Department
Cost of machinery	£42,000	£30,000
No. of employees	11	14
No. of supervisors	2	2
Floor space	6,000 sq. ft.	10,000 sq. ft.

Exhibit 3. Maximum capacity and actual/projected utilisation

	Fabrication Department (maximum available)		Assembly Department (maximum available)		Actual or anticipated usage in year
	Labour hours	Machine hours	Labour hours	Machine hours	
1986	15,000	5,900	19,000	10,100	55 per cent
1987	19,000	5,900	20,000	10,100	55 per cent
1988	19,000	5,900	24,000	10,100	85 per cent
1989	20,000	5,900	25,000	10,100	85 per cent
1990	22,000	5,900	28,000	10,100	90 per cent

meeting but I haven't got round to the detailed computations since there are so many alternatives to consider.'

After a short silence, Reynolds queried:
'Am I correct in assuming that the different methods are going to give us different overhead recovery rates?'

Niall Leonard replied:
'I'm afraid so, and I'm the person who is going to have to work them out for you!'

REQUIREMENT

1 Respond to the various arguments raised in this case study.

2 Calculate different overhead recovery rates for 1988 based on maximum, normal and expected production. Explain your figures and state which recovery rate(s) do you prefer? Why?

3 From the information calculate the approximate amount of additional production overhead attributable to the new product range. State your assumptions.

Case 3.3 Copycheck Manufacturing Company

The Copycheck Manufacturing Company makes aluminium doors and windows to order and sells them mainly to contractors in the construction industry. These frames, used in home and appartment construction, are processed through the two production departments. In the forming department, which is highly automated the raw materials are cut and shaped to the required design. In the assembly department, which is relatively labour intensive, the frames are assembled, finished and polished and are prepared for distribution.

For accounting purposes there are two service departments associated with the production function. The maintenance department carries our building and machinery repairs and general cleaning duties, and the production accounts department deals with factory payroll and production accounting records. The remaining accounting duties are carried out by a separate administration department.

Each year Copycheck develops predetermined overhead rates for its production departments which includes appropriate amounts of service department costs. These overhead rates are then applied to the various job orders in addition to direct material and direct labour costs to provide total estimated cost of production. In turn estimated costs are increased by twenty per cent to cover non-production expenses and a further fifteen per cent is added as a profit margin. The computed selling price is then discussed with the sales department before being tendered to the customer. It is usual that such quotations provide for the ability to recover from the customer cost overruns not exceeding ten per cent of quotation price.

In previous years there has been a significant amount of under and overabsorbed production overhead. The sales manager, Frank Lawlor, has pointed out that this has significant implications for selling price determination and overall company profitability.

At the annual budget meeting, the managers are anxious to determine the most appropriate method of production overhead recovery for the coming year. The company's cost accountant, Dave Murray, indicated that there were four major issues involved in determining overhead recovery rates, namely:

1   to decide whether to use a single plantwide or departmental predetermined overhead rates;
2   to determine the most appropriate method of apportioning service department costs to producing departments;
3   to select a recovery base, e.g. direct labour hours on which to recover production overheads;
4   to adopt a production volume for predetermined overhead recovery.

The meeting's chairman, managing director, Paul Phillips interupted:
'Before we get bogged down in these technical issues, can we agree
that recovery should be on the basis of full rather than variable costs?'

Frank Lawlor responded:
'I'm prepared to go along with you for the moment but we may end
up pricing ourselves out of the market.'

Lawlor had a point, since he was already aware of several 'cowboy
outfits' engaged in the manufacture of aluminium window frames who
generally quoted much lower prices than Copycheck. Nevertheless he
was reasonably happy that Copycheck offered real value to their clients.
The chairman indicated to Dave Murray to continue.

Dave, a self-styled 'whiz-kidd', was quick to seize the opportunity to
impress the meeting's participants with his technical expertise in
accounting matters. He explained:
'I've summarised all the relevant data on the following schedule
(Exhibit 1) based on both maximum and normal production. It's
highly unlikely that we could achieve anything like maximum production, but its adoption has the advantage of producing lower unit
costs, which would suit Frank. While our normal output is about
eighty-five per cent of our capacity, our current order book suggests
that we will be operating at only seventy-five per cent capacity next
year. In previous years we've used plantwide rates based on labour
hours for recovery purposes, because, honestly, I don't have the time
for anything more fancy.'

Exhibit 1.

	Forming dept.	Assembly dept.	Maintenance dept.	Production accounts
Maximum production (100 per cent)				
Factory overhead	£230,000	£65,000	£120,000	£54,000
Labour hours	38,000	15,000	31,000	13,000
Machine hours	25,000	14,000	n/a	n/a
Square feet	30,000	30,000	20,000	20,000
Employees	10	38	6	4
Normal production (eighty-five per cent)				
Factory overhead	£188,000	£49,000	£94,000	£48,000
Labour hours	30,000	10,000	19,000	9,000
Machine hours	20,000	10,000	n/a	n/a
Square feet	30,000	30,000	20,000	20,000
Employees	9	36	5	4

Sensing the time was right to press home his 'I told you so' attitude, he added:

'That graduate we took on last year as part of the Institute's training in industry programme, seems to spend half his time on study leave. When is is here, there is nothing but theory out of him. The other day he sent me an article on cost allocation and said I should read it'.

'Did you?' interjected Paul Phillips.
'I put it straight away into the bin where it belongs,' replied Murray.

The production manager, Vincent McCarthy, listened with increasing irritation to the discussion. Realising he would probably be held responsible for production overhead recovery and control, he queried the most appropriate method to use in applying service department costs to production departments in order to establish overhead absorption rates.

Dave Murray replied that the cause and effect principle indicates that the maintenance department costs should be apportioned on the basis of square feet occupied. The rationale for allocating maintenance department costs in this way would be based on the type of service rendered by this department. Since it takes maintenance personnel longer to clean and maintain physically larger departments, apportionment based on the number of square feet was logical.

He also suggested that the production accounts costs be apportioned on the basis of number of employees. In addition to payroll and accounting matters, this department does all the interviewing and testing of prospective employees in the production department. Thus cause and effect reasoning strongly indicated apportioning administration costs on the basis of the number of employees in each department.

Murray paused to light a cigarette. As he placed the match in an already overcrowded ashtray, he continued. 'To complicate matters there are different methods of apportioning service department costs to producing departments!' Vincent McCarthy asked the accountant to explain.

Dave Murray continued:
'Well there are three basic methods really. The first is the direct method which apportions service department costs to production departments only. The second method we refer to as either the step-down or the sequential method. This method recognises that some service departments provide services to other service departments, as well as to production departments, and so some service department costs can be allocated to other user service departments. The third method which we accountants refer to as the reciprocal or cross allo-

cation method, recognises full departmental interrelationships. It's very easy really!'

The production manager, growing progressively red in the face, queried whether each method would provide different overhead rates. Murray cheerfully replied, 'Of course.'

The chairman of the meeting, mindful of the impending rush hour traffic — accentuated by a bus strike — decided to close the meeting. Looking discretely at his watch, he said, 'Listen folks. I think we should adjourn the meeting until tomorrow afternoon. In the meanwhile, Dave, will you produce figures for us on overhead recovery and then we can make a more informed decision.'

The production manager readily supported the decision to adjourn, and muttered something unrepeatable about accountants under his breath.

REQUIREMENT

1   Develop overhead absorption rates for each production department. Compare your calculations with plantwide recovery rates. Explain your calculations and why you rejected various alternatives.

2   Which recovery rate(s) would you recommend? Why?

Case 3.4 Top Consulting

In 1983 Con White, the small firm's audit manager of Count and Company was invited to head up an exciting and novel project within the company. Count and Company was one of the major chartered accountancy firms operating in the city of Dublin. It was an autonomous chartered accountancy practice with no international affiliations. It had offices in some of the major towns in Ireland and provided auditing and insolvency services to business clients of all sizes.

It was obvious to all the partners of Count and Company that the majority of clients frequently requested and needed other accounting services in addition to auditing. There were many requests to provide services in relation to tax compliance and planning, management consulting, client accounting services and preparation of submissions to lending institutions. Many other chartered accountancy firms in the locality were now providing such a comprehensive service for their clients. Some years ago the local economy had experienced a recession which had two effects. First, many small businesses faced severe financial crises which placed increased emphasis on cash flow accounting and overall cost control. Second, many companies did not have adequate information systems to cope with the recessionary pressures so there was an increased demand for the provision of management accounting type services. After discussing the issue on several occasions the partners of Count and Company decided to set up a separate division within the company to provide a variety of non-auditing services to small clients. The unit would be headed by Con White and he would be solely responsible for the range of services offered and its overall profit performance. White was an accountant of vast experience and ability and had very useful contacts both within industry and government departments. He was the ideal candidate for the job and he had no hesitation in accepting the challenge.

The creation of a small business unit within Count and Company made commercial sense to everyone apart from satisfying the needs of customers. At a fundamental level it was a device for keeping staff busy who might otherwise be idle. In other words it generated contribution. Moreover a small business, with sound financial guidance, could develop into larger business concerns in future years with consequent spin-off effects for Count and Company. For example, a small firm might require immediate assistance in preparing financial projections to submit to an institution for financial funding. From this request might follow opportunities for new consulting work. In turn White was confident that consulting projects would frequently provide his unit with new chances to sell its accounting services.

The new business unit was established under the name of 'Top Consulting'. White requested and was granted his own staff who were to be entirely separate from the main auditing duties of the company. It was however possible for staff to be temporarily seconded either to or from his unit but it was agreed that such movements would be agreed by him and charged at normal commercial rates. Word of mouth, personal contacts and referrals were the primary techniques which White used to promote and develop his small business unit. Initially the firm started with just himself and an assistant, a secretary, a typewriter and an office. Now, some time later, his firm occupied a suite of office's with a total staff of eleven. White felt that the key to his success was knowing and providing exactly the type of service that the client wanted, convincing him that he needed it and then providing it. From experience he was able to estimate the amount of hours involved in any assignment and a quotation was issued on that basis. Once accepted, the quotation was never increased even though actual hours worked exceeded budgeted time. In such circumstances White would philosophically say that 'the excess cost should be charged to experience.' This was White's way of stating that cost overruns should be a lesson for all to learn. In any event such overruns tended to balance out with other jobs which were performed under budget.

Each consulting staff member of the unit was required to submit a weekly time sheet. This time report indicated the number of hours for each employee which should be charged to clients and any hours which were non-chargeable due to circumstances such as attending seminars or conferences or even idle time. When each assignment was completed the actual time spent was compared with the original time estimate. Any significant time variances were investigated and provided an 'experience base for improving predictions on future assignments.' White knew from experience that due to his fixed-price quotations' policy, profitability for his division was highly dependent on the ability to accurately predict the time taken to perform the various tasks in any consulting assignment.

For quotation purposes White worked out a 'standard rate' which he charged for each category of employee who provided consulting services to clients. Thus each category, including himself, had a different standard rate. Typically this standard rate represented the actual salary of staff in addition to a sum consisting of overheads and profit target. The estimated number of hours to be worked by each employee on a consulting assignment would be multiplied by the standard rate for that employee to determine the charge to the client. White did not make price concessions to clients by taking into consideration 'busy' or 'slack' times or whether a cheap quotation had the potential to generate future revenue. There was a 'going rate' for the services provided and White was not prepared to negotiate on the matter. While he never said it to clients, White had the attitude 'if you need to know how much it costs, you probably can't afford it.' In any event he disliked negotiations on money matters. In addition to the quoted price for the job the client would automatically be charged for specific outlay such as hotel accommodation.

In an attempt to establish standard hourly rates for each category of staff next year White made the following cost estimates for staff together with a projection of chargeable time (Exhibit 1).

Exhibit 1. Projected consulting staff costs and chargeable hours

Staff category and numbers	Annual salary	Holiday entitlements	Actual work time (chargeable percentage)
Managing director (Con White)	£25,000	4 weeks	70 per cent
Seniors (4)	£18,000 each	3 weeks	90 per cent
Junior Assistants (4)	£7,000 each	2 weeks	60 per cent

White accepted that he would have relatively low chargeable hours next year since he was involved in various committees of the local institute and was also vice-captain of the golf club. The seniors would be able to charge out virtually all their hours worked since, being qualified personnel, they could be considered independent work units. The junior assistants were more problematic since, being unqualified, they were unable to exercise a great deal of initiative in some circumstances. In addition they were frequently absent from work due to extensive study and examination leave.

There were several other expenses which needed to be considered. There were two secretaries employed at an annual salary of £8,000 each and who were entitled to three weeks' annual holidays. In addition, general overheads which included stationery, telephone and building expenses were estimated to increase by ten per cent on last year's level of £22,000. Moreover, the firm was obliged to make social welfare contributions on behalf of each employee, including White. The basic contribution rate was twelve per cent of basic salary but this was only payable on salary up to £14,000 per annum. In addition the company was committed to fund a pension scheme for White and his four seniors equivalent to five per cent of basic salary. After providing for all these costs White was anxious that his consulting business generate an annual profit of £32,000.

Before White had the opportunity to perform any calculations he reread a memorandum which he had dictated the previous day. The memorandum (Exhibit 2) summarises the estimated time taken for a prospective consulting assignment. The assignment, to take place early in the new year, is for a new client that White is interested in acquiring.

Exhibit 2. Summary of hours required for job: ABC Ltd

Staff category	Total hours engaged
Managing director	24 hours
Seniors	120 hours
Junior assistants	42 hours
Outlay (hotel accommodation)	£3,100

Based on the information he had gathered, White has to decide on a quotation price for the prospective consulting assignment.

REQUIREMENT

1   Prepare a full quotation for Job-ABC Ltd., assuming the standard chargeout rate is computed separately for each category of consulting staff. Justify your figures.

2   What do you consider to be the minimum price which *could* be charged for this job? Explain.

3   What annual sales revenue at normal chargeout rates will provide a profit target of £32,000 for the forthcoming year. Explain your calculations.

Case 3.5 Home Furniture Limited

It was not the type of assignment for which Kevin Byrne would have volunteered had he been given the choice. However he felt obliged to help out his old school pal, John Davis, who was the owner and manager of Home Furniture. Since leaving school the two pals had lost contact with each other. Kevin concentrated on his accounting studies whereas John pursued a career in art and design. Now, several years later they met by chance in a pub after a football international. Initially they traded anecdotes about the 'old days' before updating themselves on each other's current careers.

Kevin had since qualified as an accountant and was doing very well. John had spent several years acquiring expertise in the design of quality home furniture. Thereafter he put his expertise to the test and set up a small manufacturing operation. From modest beginnings the company had grown to a size where several production personnel were employed together with a small administrative staff. Unfortunately Home Furniture could not afford the services of a full time accountant. The end result, admitted Davis, was that the accounting records were in a 'frightful mess' and personally, he was too busy on the production side to rectify matters.

The company made several varieties of quality home furniture to order including tables, chairs and bookshelves. The orders came mainly from large department stores. Earlier this year Home Furniture had entered into a number of large contracts with several department stores requiring the production of different units with an agreed production quota per month. At first sight the contracts appeared lucrative in terms of agreed price compared with estimated costings. However since non-delivery of monthly production quotas would result in a fine being imposed on Davis by the retail stores, his production staff often had to work overtime in order to complete certain jobs on time. This was expensive, Davis explained, since the basic labour rate was £10 per hour with overtime being paid at a premium of fifty per cent. His basic production problem, Davis acknowledged, was general lack of capacity which placed him in a 'catch-22' situation. His current lack of capacity necessitated overtime on many orders. Yet if he expanded and acquired additional capacity he could be forced to continue trading with the large department stores, but perhaps on their terms which could be less attractive than current conditions. Since the accounting records were disorganised Davis didn't even know which orders were profitable. After further discussion and persuasion Byrne agreed to help his old pal and promised to pay a visit to the factory the following Saturday.

Byrne arrived early next Saturday morning at the prearranged time and took up temporary residence in Davis' office which was littered with files, furniture, account books and paper. Byrne opened the window to let some fresh air in.

After reviewing the post-match celebrations of the previous Saturday Davis explained that he had set a profit target of £10,000 for the last six months of trading. He didn't know if it had been achieved but had a gut feeling that he was off the mark and on the wrong side at that. He had no idea which orders were profitable and which weren't.

'I've got everything here for you,' said Davis. 'Probably the best place for you to start is with our financial position at the end of last year.' He pointed to a large file on the edge of the desk.

The front page represented the company's opening trial balance with supporting schedules (Exhibit 1). 'This is very helpful,' commented Byrne.

Exhibit 1. Trial Balance at 31 December 1987

	Debit	Credit
Fixed assets (net)	£20,000	
Raw materials control	25,000	
Work in progress (Note 1)	17,400	
Share capital		£24,000
Retained profits		13,000
Bank overdraft		29,000
Debtors	20,600	
Creditors		18,000
Production overhead due		2,000
Administration expenses prepaid	3,000	
	86,000	86,000

Note 1 Analysis of work in progress.

Job No.	Materials	Labour	Production overhead
87–92	£1,000	£3,400	£1,700
87–98	2,000	6,200	3,100
	3,000	9,600	4,800

Davis then briefly explained the nature of his manufacturing operation. Typically the buyer from a department store would visit Davis in his office and discuss a possible production order, its feasability and delivery dates. Once broad agreement was reached on these issues a detailed quotation was sought. Davis would estimate the type and specific amount of materials required for each job. The material estimating process was relatively simple and usually accurate. This was because if a client wanted, say, a bookshelf, the required amount of wood could be gauged accurately. Material wastage was negligible since the workforce consisted mainly of skilled workers. Likewise labour requirements were fairly easily calculated since most of the work involved could be estimated from previous orders. Production overhead was recovered at the rate of thirty per cent of basic labour cost (excluding overtime) and twenty per cent was then added to total production cost to cover administration costs and leave a reasonable profit margin.

Byrne then picked up the job cost file which showed the amount of materials requisitioned and labour hours worked on each job during the past six months (Exhibit 2). The direct materials figure had been obtained from material requisitions' dockets which had to be completed before material was issued for production. These dockets showed the amount and price of materials required for each job. The total labour hours worked was obtained from job cards which all production employees were obliged to complete each week.

Exhibit 2. Usage of direct materials and direct labour (Jan-June 1988)

Quotation Price	Job no.	Direct materials	Basic labour hours	Overtime labour hours
£10,000	87–92	—	100	14
15,000	87–98	—	60	nil
25,000	88–1	3,500	1,000	250
32,000	88–2	5,400	1,400	nil
20,000	89–3	2,500	700	120
35,000	88–4	4,250	1,500	200
55,000	88–5	6,400	2,600	nil
60,000	Various (minor)	7,000	2,700	200

Byrne asked to see any other documents or information, especially in relation to cash movements, goods purchased and sold. After some delay Davis produced a summary for the past six months (Exhibit 3).

Exhibit 3.

Raw material purchase invoices	£35,000
Invoices for production overhead expenses incurred	£28,000
Administration expenses incurred	£31,000
Payments to creditors for materials and expenses	£85,000
Wages paid	
Basic (11,000 hours)	£110,000
Overtime (850 hours)	£12,750
Receipts from debtors	£200,000

Davis indicated that there were a few other pieces of information which may be useful. All work performed during the six months had been completed with the exception of job No. 88–5 which was still in progress. The completed work had all been delivered to customers and invoiced although payments from some customers were outstanding.

121

Byrne then queried depreciation policy in relation to fixed assets. 'We depreciate our assets by £4,000 a year,' replied Davis. He added, 'I hoped you have enough information to build up some sort of financial picture of the company for the past six months. Your observations of what we're doing right or wrong in financial terms would be much appreciated. I'll leave you alone.' Davis departed from his office and quietly closed the door.

A quick review by Byrne confirmed that he had sufficient information, admittedly not verified by him, to construct a crude set of accounts for the period and extract some basic management accounting information. The first thing he noticed was that the firm's bank overdraft had increased to £36,750. Not a significant increase, thought Byrne but perhaps its trend was indicative of the general state of the company. Byrne realised that Davis would require not just figures but recommendations as well.

REQUIREMENT

1 Record the above information in the cost ledger of Home Furniture Limited and prepare a profit and loss account for the six months ended 30 June 1988. Defend your treatment of overtime premiums and the under/over absorbed production overhead.

2 With hindsight, what predetermined overhead recovery rates should Davis have used during the six months' period? Why?

3 Prepare a schedule comparing the quotation price of each job with the actual cost incurred. What do your figures reveal?

4 What general or specific recommendations would you make to Davis?

Case 3.6 Lynch Printers

Dermot Lynch is the owner and managing director of a small printing business bearing his name. The company undertakes each printing job according to special instructions received from the customer. The types of printing orders include cards, invitations, small books and even occasional trade magazines. The nature of the printing business virtually ensures that there is no closing stock of finished goods on hand at the end of any accounting period. Work is done according to customer orders received or not at all. Sales and purchase invoices were paid on delivery so that the working capital investment in the company was virtually negligible.

According to the financial results for 1987, the accounting year just ended, Lynch Printers had returned a net loss for the first time in its history. The loss was not of alarming proportions but Lynch wondered what had gone wrong and what he could do about it. Logic suggested that his problems were due to either low prices or excessive costs, but this puzzled Lynch since each job was priced to include all costs to which a satisfactory profit margin was added. Moreover costs did not appear to have increased compared with previous years.

Lynch Printers had developed a good reputation in the trade for quality work and reliability of delivery. Lynch passionately believed that these two factors were crucial in determining the success of his business. Quotation price was very much of secondary importance. Over the years his customers had continually insisted on good quality work and adherence to agreed delivery dates. For guarantees on these two issues the customer was willing to pay any price within reasonable bounds.

Lynch Printers use a system recommended by his trade association to quote a price for each printing job. When the customer specifies the type of work required, Lynch establishes an estimated cost for the job which includes direct and indirect expenses. A fixed percentage (ten per cent) is added to total cost for profit and the final figure is given to the customer as a quotation. The quotation price as far as Lynch is concerned, is 'not-negotiable'. Thus there are no special prices for any jobs. It's a take it or leave it situation as far as Lynch is concerned. If accepted by the customer it becomes a fixed price so that any cost overruns are absorbed by the printers and are not passed on to customers. This quotation system has been in operation for several years and Lynch prided himself on his estimating ability. Moreover it was a rare occurrence for a customer not to accept the quoted price. Admittedly, the absence of other printing firms in the locality meant that potential customers were placed at a slight disadvantage when dealing with Lynch.

The production process in Lynch Printers was relatively simple.

Initially Lynch consulted his production manager about the feasibility of the order including the size and styles of type to be used. Once agreement was reached and the order confirmed by the customer Lynch issued a production order, which included printing instructions, and the material was sent to the composing room, where it was set in type. A galley proof was printed and sent to the copy editor who checked it against the original material. Any errors were marked on the proof which was then sent to the customer for approval. When returned by the customer the appropriate corrections were made and the order was then sent to the pressroom for production. Copies were then printed, bound and packaged for delivery to the customer.

The direct expenses of the business consisted of the cost of paper used and actual labour hours worked on each printing job. All other expenses were classified as overhead. Lynch Printers currently employ six individuals in the production process. They work a maximum of thirty-five hours per week, forty-eight weeks per year with four weeks' holiday entitlement. Because of space limitations no more than six typesetters may be employed at any one time. The company has recently introduced the practice of 'flexitime' which has improved work practices enormously and has eliminated the necessity for overtime. For example if an employee takes Monday morning off he will work late some other evening, at no additional cost, to make up lost time.

For quotation purposes the total number of labour hours required in typesetting and printing for each job is estimated by Lynch and is priced at actual cost of labour work to be performed. To this computed labour cost a predetermined percentage is added to cover general production overhead costs, non-chargeable labour hours and also administration and delivery costs.

The other direct cost is that of paper. It is fairly easy to estimate the amount of paper required for each job since the customer specifies the size of the paper required, e.g. A4 size. In addition the quality of paper to be used is agreed in advance with the customer. Lynch personally discusses such requirements with each customer and offers advice. They

Exhibit 1. Income summary for year ended 31 December 1986

Sales		£226,900
Direct costs:		
Cost of paper consumed	£22,000	
Wages (directly charged out)	90,720	
Overheads:		
Consumables (not directly chargeable)	4,400	
Wages (not directly chargeable)	18,480	
General production overheads, administration and delivery.	72,240	207,840
Net profit		19,060

normally accept his recommendation and are ultimately more than pleased with the completed product. To the estimated cost of paper used is added a predetermined percentage to cover 'consumables' such as ink and other minor costs incidental to the production process.

The predetermined percentages to recover both production overheads, administration, delivery and non-chargeable wages and consumables are always set equivalent to the actual percentage relationships between corresponding costs incurred during the previous financial year. In effect last year's actual cost performance becomes the budget for the following year. While this basis may compound any inefficiencies within the production process it has the advantage of considerably simplifying the accounting calculations. A summary of the actual results for 1986 which formed the basis for 1987 estimates is provided in Exhibit 1.

Comparing the 1986 profit performance with the loss incurred in 1987, Lynch was even more puzzled especially since there were no cost increases over the two years. He knew however that in 1987 business had fallen — measured in terms of chargeable labour hours. In 1986, ninety per cent of the labour hours worked were charged to specific jobs. However in 1987 only seventy-five per cent of hours worked represented chargeable hours. Even though the volume of trade had dropped no one had been laid off since good typesetters and printers were difficult to recruit and volume might improve in following years.

The actual general production overheads including administration and delivery costs amounted to £72,240 in 1987. Lynch was not surprised that they were the same as the previous year since they were predominantly fixed in nature. The cost of paper consumed during 1987 amounted to £19,000. At least it was less than last year, Lynch consoled himself, as was the £3,500 incurred on consumables.

As always it was necessary to obtain reliable data on what had actually happened during the year in order to analyse the situation, Lynch thought to himself. Once obtained, he could begin to draw conclusions and implications. Even at this preliminary stage Lynch anticipated that his whole basis of pricing policy might be in need of revision for 1988.

REQUIREMENT

1 What were the recovery rates used in 1987 for both consumables and production overhead? Use these rates and other actual data to calculate actual sales for 1987.

2 What was the amount of the loss for 1987? Explain how the loss has arisen. Comment critically on Lynch's pricing system.

3 Prepare a statement comparing actual performance in 1987 from budget. What information content do these variances have? Justify your choice of budget figures.

Case 3.7 Beechcroft Limited

The managing director of Beechcroft Limited was a little puzzled as he re-examined his firm's summary income statement for the quarter ended December 1988. Ralph McMahon had taken over as managing director of the company, then unprofitable, over a year ago with the express intention of reversing its fortunes. The company produced a single product. At the beginning of the current year the company had no opening stock so McMahon quickly implemented an expansionary production programme. Production output exceeded sales volume for the first three-quarters of the year.

Maximum capacity at the plant was 5,000 units per quarter but in previous years this had rarely been obtained. Rather the company would normally operate at about sixty per cent capacity. Gradually the company's fortunes, as a result of expanding sales and effective cost control, was beginning to improve, if the cash flow position was anything to go by. Sales in the final quarter of the year were £80,000 up on the previous quarter, so McMahon was expecting his income statement to show a reasonable increase in profit. However he had just received an income summary from the company accountant which showed a small increase in profit compared with the previous quarter. Unable to conceal his disappointment McMahon telephoned his accountant for an explanation.

McMahon had difficulty in contacting his accountant. Paddy Hunt, since his phone was continuously engaged — or deliberately left off the hook. Eventually McMahon made contact and asked Hunt if there was any possibility of a mistake in the accounts. 'Absolutely none,' assured Hunt. 'The basic problem,' continued Hunt 'was that that the company sold a lot of stock in the recent quarter which was produced during previous quarters and that resulted in significant decline in stock levels.'

McMahon was even more confused. He queried, 'are you saying that the reason for our poor profit performance this quarter is because we sold too much stock? Or putting it another way, do I understand that if we had sold less during the period, our profits would have been higher?

"You're oversimplifying things. The reason why our profit increase is relatively small is due to our accounting system really. You see, we operate an absorption costing system which means that a portion of our production overheads are attributed to closing stock at the end of each quarter. In previous quarters there was a gradual stock build up and so more and more of our production costs were being carried over to following accounting periods. Last quarter we eventually managed to dispose a large portion of our accumulated stock build up and our profits do not adequately reflect our increased sales.'

McMahon was still unbelieving. He retorted, 'Does this mean that in previous periods when output exceed sales, our profits were too high?'

Without hesitating Hunt replied, 'In a manner of speaking.'

McMahon continued, 'I understand what you're saying but don't understand how this can happen. O.K., so you can explain it by way of accounting conventions but surely it's illogical. Common sense dictates to me that when sales go up, and costs remain reasonably stable, profits should reflect increased sales. What's the point trying to increase sales? That is what we have achieved during the last quarter and our income statement should show it. Can you come up to my office as soon as you can so that we can discuss the matter further. Bring some figures with you.

Some time later Hunt arrived in McMahon's office and seated himself in the most confortable chair. McMahon queried briefly, 'Is there anything we can do or what would you recommend.'

'Well,' responded Hunt. 'I've been asking myself the same question. We can look at the problem from a different angle and in effect change our accounting system. We could move from absorption costing to a variable production costing system. In that way our profits should relate better to sales.'

It was obvious that McMahon was interested in this proposal since he sat forward in his chair and put his elbows on his large mahogany desk. 'Tell me more,' he requested.

'The two alternative accounting methods differ only in respect of fixed production overhead,' stated Hunt. 'If we switch to a variable costing system all fixed production overhead will be charged in a lump sum to our profit and loss account each quarter rather than apportioning some of it to closing stock. In other words we would treat our fixed production overheads in exactly the same manner as administration expenses. As a result there would be no problem with under or overapplied production overhead. In addition our stock valuation procedure would be considerably simplified as would some of our financial projections for each quarter. In fact it would simplify the accounting system considerably since we would no longer have to allocate fixed production overhead to our product. My work load would be reduced and as a consequence I could get out the quarterly accounts much more quickly.'

McMahon was impressed at Hunt's proposal. While he did not understand the mechanics of the proposal he understood its important implication, namely that profits would relate to sales rather than production output. 'How would your figures for last quarter be affected?' queried McMahon as he glanced at Hunt's summary for that period (Exhibit 1).

'I'd have to take some time to work that out,' responded Hunt. He added, 'You will notice that our average production cost had reduced considerably during the year. This calculation was based on actual

Exhibit 1. Operating summary for year ended 31 December, 1988.

Quarter	Production (units)	Sales revenue	Average unit production cost	Total non-production cost
1	2,000	£50,000	£44	£22,000
2	2,000	100,000	£44	£26,000
3	3,600	150,000	£28	£30,000
4	3,000	230,000	£32	£36,400

output levels and it includes both fixed and variable production costs. However the variable production cost per unit was constant during the period, largely as a result of effective cost control and also because each unit produced required exactly one hour of machine processing time. Non-production costs comprise administration costs which were fixed in nature and sales commission. Sales commission at the rate of £4 per unit sold was payable. I'll get the revised figures to you as soon as possible and then you can make a final decision,' he concluded.

McMahon responded, 'If what you say is true, I don't need to see your figures before deciding. I've decided. Let's do it.'

'Its not quite that simple,' replied Hunt. 'You see, our financial accounts must be prepared in accordance with recognised accounting standards issued by the accountancy profession. The standard dealing with stock valuation specifically requires that we retain our existing system of absorption costing. Our financial statements are presented at the AGM and are given to our bankers and the tax authorities. If we didn't comply with accounting standards the users would become very suspicious. What we could do is adopt a new system for our own internal purposes and retain the current system for external parties.'

McMahon interjected, 'Does that mean that we'll have two sets of accounts for the same quarter showing two different profit figures? And, if that's the case the bank will get the "bad" set and we keep the "good" set?' Sounds a crazy thing to me! I've heard of "cooking the books" but doing it to your own disadvantage is a bit stupid.'

'Well there is a complicating factor to consider,' responded Hunt. 'If we keep our profits low, we may be able to reduce our tax bill and more importantly restrain the unions from seeking higher wage increases.'

'What you're saying is that your proposal may not be such a good idea after all', responded McMahon by way of statement rather than question.

'I'll tell you what I can do,' said Hunt. 'There is a formula which allows one to compute very quickly the profit figure under both systems. I'll send it to you with all my figures. We can then have another discussion.'

That evening McMahon received the following memorandum from Hunt (Exhibit 2).

Exhibit 2.

To: Ralph McMahon
From: Paddy Hunt
Re: Proposed switch from absorption to variable production costing.

The following formulae will help in your deliberations. The first formula allows you to quickly calculate net profit under the proposed variable production costing method. The second formula allows you to calculate the different profit levels between the two methods.

1 $\qquad$ $Pv = Y.C - [F - O]$

2 $\qquad$ $Pv-Pa = F/N \ (Y - X)$

where $\quad$ Pv $\ =$ net profit under variable production costing
$\qquad$ Pa $\ =$ net profit under absorption costing
$\qquad$ Y $\ \ =$ units sold
$\qquad$ C $\ \ =$ contribution margin per unit
$\qquad$ F $\ \ =$ total fixed production costs
$\qquad$ O $\ \ =$ total of non-production costs
$\qquad$ N $\ \ =$ normal production capacity
$\qquad$ X $\ \ =$ units produced

As yet I haven't had the time to work out the exact figures for the last quarter but hope to have them shortly.

REQUIREMENT

1   Which costing system do you recommend? Why?

2   Using variable production costing, prepare a profit statement for each of the four quarters.

3   Prepare a profit statement for the four quarters using an absorption costing system. Clearly indicate the amount of under/over recovery of overhead. To what extent have under/over recovery of fixed production variances got relevance for planning and controlling the enterprise?

4   What sales level would provide an annual profit target of £50,000? Explain your calculations.

Appendices

APPENDIX 1

Critical values of the t-distribution

Degrees of freedom	Ninety-nine per cent confidence interval t.01	Ninety-five per cent confidence interval t.025	Ninety per cent confidence interval t.05
1	31.821	12.706	6.314
2	6.965	4.303	2.920
3	4.541	3.182	2.353
4	3.747	2.776	2.132
5	3.365	2.571	2.015
6	3.143	2.447	1.943
7	2.998	2.365	1.895
8	2.896	2.306	1.860
9	2.821	2.262	1.833
10	2.764	2.228	1.812
11	2.718	2.201	1.796
12	2.681	2.179	1.782
13	2.650	2.160	1.771
14	2.624	2.145	1.761
15	2.602	2.131	1.753
16	2.583	2.120	1.746
17	2.567	2.110	1.740
18	2.552	2.101	1.734
19	2.539	2.093	1.729
20	2.528	2.086	1.725
21	2.518	2.080	1.721
22	2.508	2.074	1.717
23	2.500	2.069	1.714
24	2.492	2.064	1.711
25	2.485	2.060	1.708
26	2.479	2.056	1.706
27	2.473	2.052	1.703
28	2.467	2.048	1.701
29	2.462	2.045	1.699
inf.	2.326	1.960	1.645

APPENDIX 2
Area under the standard normal curve

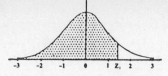

Z	0.00	0.01	0.02	0.03	0.04	0.05	0.06	0.07	0.08	0.09
0·0	0·5000	5040	5080	5120	5160	5199	5239	5279	5319	5359
0·1	0·5398	5438	5478	5517	5557	5596	5636	5675	5714	5753
0·2	0·5793	5832	5871	5910	5948	5987	6026	6064	6103	6141
0·3	0·6179	6217	6255	6293	6331	6368	6406	6443	6480	6517
0·4	0·6554	6591	6628	6664	6700	6736	6772	6808	6844	6879
0·5	0·6915	6950	6985	7019	7054	7088	7123	7157	7190	7224
0·6	0·7257	7291	7324	7357	7389	7422	7454	7486	7517	7549
0·7	0·7580	7611	7642	7673	7704	7734	7764	7794	7823	7852
0·8	0·7881	7910	7939	7967	7995	8023	8051	8078	8106	8133
0·9	0·8159	8186	8212	8238	8264	8289	8315	8340	8365	8389
1·0	0·8413	8438	8461	8485	8508	8531	8554	8577	8599	8621
1·1	0·8643	8665	8686	8708	8729	8749	8770	8790	8810	8830
1·2	0·8849	8869	8888	8907	8925	8944	8962	8980	8997	9015
1·3	0·9032	9049	9066	9082	9099	9115	9131	9147	9162	9177
1·4	0·9192	9207	9222	9236	9251	9265	9279	9292	9306	9319
1·5	0·9332	9345	9357	9370	9382	9394	9406	9418	9429	9441
1·6	0·9452	9463	9474	9484	9495	9505	9515	9525	9535	9545
1·7	0·9554	9564	9573	9582	9591	9599	9608	9616	9625	9633
1·8	0·9641	9649	9656	9664	9671	9678	9686	9693	9699	9706
1·9	0·9713	9719	9726	9732	9738	9744	9750	9756	9761	9767
2·0	0·9772	9778	9783	9788	9793	9798	9803	9808	9812	9817
2·1	0·9821	9826	9830	9834	9838	9842	9846	9850	9854	9857
2·2	0·9861	9864	9868	9871	9875	9878	9881	9884	9887	9890
2·3	0·9893	9896	9898	9901	9904	9906	9909	9911	9913	9916
2·4	0·9918	9920	9922	9925	9927	9929	9931	9932	9934	9936
2·5	0·99379	99396	99413	99430	99446	99461	99477	99492	99506	99520
2·6	0·99534	99547	99560	99573	99585	99598	99609	99621	99632	99643
2·7	0·99653	99664	99674	99683	99693	99702	99711	99720	99728	99736
2·8	0·99744	99752	99760	99767	99774	99781	99788	99795	99801	99807
2·9	0·99813	99819	99825	99831	99836	99841	99846	99851	99856	99861
3·0	0·99865	99869	99874	99878	99882	99886	99889	99893	99897	99900
3·1	0·99903	99906	99910	99913	99916	99918	99921	99924	99926	99929
3·2	0·99931	99934	99936	99938	99940	99942	99944	99946	99948	99950
3·3	0·99952	99953	99955	99957	99958	99960	99961	99962	99964	99965
3·4	0·99966	99968	99969	99970	99971	99972	99973	99974	99975	99976
3·5	0·99977	99978	99978	99979	99980	99981	99981	99982	99983	99983
3·6	0·99984	99985	99985	99986	99986	99987	99987	99988	99988	99989
3·7	0·99989	99990	99990	99990	99991	99991	99992	99992	99992	99992
3·8	0·99993	99993	99993	99994	99994	99994	99994	99995	99995	99995
3·9	0·99995	99995	99996	99996	99996	99996	99996	99996	99997	99997

APPENDIX 3

Discount tables

Present Value of £1

Years hence	1%	2%	4%	6%	8%	10%	12%	14%	15%	16%	18%	20%	22%	24%	25%	26%	28%	30%	35%	40%	45%	50%
1	.990	.980	.962	.943	.926	.909	.893	.877	.870	.862	.847	.833	.820	.806	.800	.794	.781	.769	.741	.714	.690	.666
2	.980	.961	.925	.890	.857	.826	.797	.769	.756	.743	.718	.694	.672	.650	.640	.630	.610	.592	.549	.510	.476	.444
3	.971	.942	.889	.840	.794	.751	.712	.675	.658	.641	.608	.579	.551	.524	.512	.500	.477	.455	.406	.364	.328	.296
4	.961	.924	.855	.792	.735	.683	.636	.592	.572	.552	.516	.482	.451	.423	.410	.397	.373	.350	.301	.260	.226	.197
5	.951	.906	.822	.747	.681	.621	.567	.519	.497	.476	.437	.402	.370	.341	.328	.315	.291	.269	.223	.186	.156	.131
6	.942	.888	.790	.705	.630	.564	.507	.456	.432	.410	.370	.335	.303	.275	.262	.250	.227	.207	.165	.133	.108	.088
7	.933	.871	.760	.665	.583	.513	.452	.400	.376	.354	.314	.279	.249	.222	.210	.198	.178	.159	.122	.095	.074	.058
8	.923	.853	.731	.627	.540	.467	.404	.351	.327	.305	.266	.233	.204	.179	.168	.157	.139	.123	.091	.068	.051	.039
9	.914	.837	.703	.592	.500	.424	.361	.308	.284	.263	.225	.194	.167	.144	.134	.125	.108	.094	.067	.048	.035	.026
10	.905	.820	.676	.558	.463	.386	.322	.270	.247	.227	.191	.162	.137	.116	.107	.099	.085	.073	.050	.035	.024	.017
11	.896	.804	.650	.527	.429	.350	.287	.237	.215	.195	.162	.135	.112	.094	.086	.079	.066	.056	.037	.025	.017	.011
12	.887	.788	.625	.497	.397	.319	.257	.208	.187	.168	.137	.112	.092	.076	.069	.062	.052	.043	.027	.018	.012	.008
13	.879	.773	.601	.469	.368	.290	.229	.182	.163	.145	.116	.093	.075	.061	.055	.050	.040	.033	.020	.013	.008	.005
14	.870	.758	.577	.442	.340	.263	.205	.160	.141	.125	.099	.078	.062	.049	.044	.039	.032	.025	.015	.009	.006	.003
15	.861	.743	.555	.417	.315	.239	.183	.140	.123	.108	.084	.065	.051	.040	.035	.031	.025	.020	.011	.006	.004	.002
16	.853	.728	.534	.394	.292	.218	.163	.123	.107	.093	.071	.054	.042	.032	.028	.025	.019	.015	.008	.005	.003	.002
17	.844	.714	.513	.371	.270	.198	.146	.108	.093	.080	.060	.045	.034	.026	.023	.020	.015	.012	.006	.003	.002	.001
18	.836	.700	.494	.350	.250	.180	.130	.095	.081	.069	.051	.038	.028	.021	.018	.016	.012	.009	.005	.002	.001	.001
19	.828	.686	.475	.331	.232	.164	.116	.083	.070	.060	.043	.031	.023	.017	.014	.012	.009	.007	.003	.002	.001	
20	.820	.673	.456	.312	.215	.149	.104	.073	.061	.051	.037	.026	.019	.014	.012	.010	.007	.005	.002	.001	.001	
21	.811	.660	.439	.294	.199	.135	.093	.064	.053	.044	.031	.022	.015	.011	.009	.008	.006	.004	.002	.001		
22	.803	.647	.422	.278	.184	.123	.083	.056	.046	.038	.026	.018	.013	.009	.007	.006	.004	.003	.001	.001		
23	.795	.634	.406	.262	.170	.112	.074	.049	.040	.033	.022	.015	.010	.007	.006	.005	.003	.002	.001			
24	.788	.622	.390	.247	.158	.102	.066	.043	.035	.028	.019	.013	.008	.006	.005	.004	.003	.002	.001			
25	.780	.610	.375	.233	.146	.092	.059	.038	.030	.024	.016	.010	.007	.005	.004	.003	.002	.001	.001			
26	.772	.598	.361	.220	.135	.084	.053	.033	.026	.021	.014	.009	.006	.004	.003	.002	.002	.001				
27	.764	.586	.347	.207	.125	.076	.047	.029	.023	.018	.011	.007	.005	.003	.002	.002	.001	.001				
28	.757	.574	.333	.196	.116	.069	.042	.026	.020	.016	.010	.006	.004	.002	.002	.002	.001	.001				
29	.749	.563	.321	.185	.107	.063	.037	.022	.017	.014	.008	.005	.003	.002	.002	.001	.001	.001				
30	.742	.552	.308	.174	.099	.057	.033	.020	.015	.012	.007	.004	.003	.002	.001	.001	.001	.001				
40	.672	.453	.208	.097	.046	.022	.011	.005	.004	.003	.001	.001										
50	.608	.372	.141	.054	.021	.009	.003	.001	.001	.001